KNOW THIS...
From Torments to Miracles

Jim Hnatiuk

PEOPLE WHO KNOW JIM HNATIUK

 I've had the pleasure of knowing Jim Hnatiuk and working with him for more than a decade, and we remain personal friends. In all the years I've known him, many characteristics greatly impressed me: I know him to be scrupulously honest; a gentleman; and a trustworthy friend. Most relevant to this book, however, is his meticulous attention to accuracy and detail—probably the reason he was able to earn the highest non-commissioned rank in the Canadian Navy. That accuracy is reflected in this report of his personal life experiences. Much of what I read in this book came as a surprise to me—but I believe every word, because I know the author's integrity. What you'll read reveals very personal details of his private life; but it's presented for your benefit. I hope and pray that multitudes will read this remarkable narrative; and above all, that you'll apply its lessons to your own life. The rewards for doing so will amply repay the effort. This book can change your life—for the better.

Mr. Ron O. Gray
Editorial Columnist, Journalist, Public Relations

 Jim Hnatiuk is a trusted leader and has provided sage advice, guidance and exceptional service to our church fellowship for over a decade. His book, *Know This...From Torments to Miracles* is a deep personal account of an eye-opening, life-altering journey. Drawing extensively on his personal experiences, Jim offers a vulnerable and honest account of being released from the shackles that have chained him for years. Jim's ability to transcend evil of every kind is powerfully presented. This thoroughly grounded and altogether responsible advice exposes a transformational encounter that is out of this world. Read it and be changed!

The Rev Dr. Lennett J. Anderson CD
Senior Pastor, Emmanuel Baptist Church

 Jim Hnatiuk has bravely given us a picture of the ugliness and deception of the realm of spiritual darkness through his own personal experiences. This account reveals a direct attempt to bring a human being into an ongoing relationship with the world of darkness. The demonic world, as he demonstrated, gives us a picture of some of the deceptions used by Satan. This book will not only help you to recognize light from darkness, but how to use that light ("I Am Who I Am") to overcome your darkness.

The Hon. Larry Spencer
Member of the 37th Parliament of Canada
Author, **Sacrificed? Truth or Politics**

 I have known Jim Hnatiuk for over 20 years, and he has proven to be a man of incredible integrity and dedication to serving others. It is therefore my privilege to recommend this book to those seeking to be challenged, and to grow in their under-standing of overcoming the challenges of life. This autobiography from Jim both challenges us and reminds us that there is an unseen battle going on for the very souls of all people. For those many men and women across all walks of life who are struggling with a wide variety of issues, this book and its insights will provide guidance, hope and inspiration that change and freedom is possible.

Lt. Commander Harold King CD

Marilyn
Warwick

KN**O**W THIS...
From TORMENTS to MIRACLES

JIM HNATIUK

Guardian
B O O K S

Belleville, Ontario, Canada

ISBN: 978-1-4600-0622-1
LSI Edition: 978-1-4600-0623-8
E-book ISBN: 978-1-4600-0624-5
(E-book available from the Kindle Store, KOBO and the iBooks Store)

Cataloguing data available from Library and Archives Canada

To order additional copies, visit:
www.TormentsToMiracles.com
www.essencebookstore.com

To contact the author:
contact@TormentsToMiracles.com
www.TormentsToMiracles.com

Guardian Books is an imprint of *Essence Publishing*.
For more information, contact:
20 Hanna Court, Belleville, Ontario, Canada K8P 5J2
Phone: 1-800-238-6376 • Fax: (613) 962-3055
Email: info@essence-publishing.com
Web site: www.essence-publishing.com

Printed in Canada
by

This book is dedicated to
My wife Ellen, who is beautiful inside and out

Our wonderful son and daughter, Douglas and Carlleen,
their spouses, Jennie and Derek, and

Our treasured grandchildren,
Jaedon, Linden, Anderson, Greyson, and
All those that follow…

*"So That All May **Know This** Truth"*

ACKNOWLEDGEMENTS

With the sincerest of intentions,
I'd like to acknowledge all my brothers and sisters.
I love them and my heart goes out to each of them.
They have their own life story;
this book only has to do with mine.

I thank God for my biological mother and father
who brought me into this world.
Regardless of what I've shared in this book,
I love them both, and nothing will ever change that.

ABOUT THE AUTHOR

This book will reveal to you more about this author
than any biography could ever hope to achieve.

CONTENTS

CHAPTER ONE

Know This Preamble

The one important thing I am attempting in writing this book is to put to the best use possible what I've experienced and learned in my sixty-five years, so others may benefit from this knowledge. You can be assured that I'm not writing to seek sympathy nor some type of self gratification; that would be a tragic waste of my time and yours. This book will not be a waste of your time, if you commit yourself to reading it to the end—and then put some of this information to the test so that you to can greatly benefit as I did.

In public speaking engagements over the past decade, I've been able to share snippets of these astonishing life experiences, and I've been told that even those talks have helped many come to a better understanding of some of the phenomena and/or life struggles that they and/or their loved ones are suffering through. Many suddenly realize that there *is* hope, when they thought they had lost all hope. Therefore I'm confident that those reading this more detailed account will most assuredly benefit more after knowing the complete story. Don't get hung up on any particular chapter; make a commitment to

> *"Many suddenly realize that there is hope, when they thought they had lost all hope."*

see this to the end—because, believe me, there is a force that will be trying to convince you to do otherwise.

There are a couple of important preambles that should be clearly understood by those choosing to read these life chronicles.

First, to adequately capture the true magnitude and the intensity of the supernatural experiences described in this book, I'm sure my command of the English language must be lacking; and in some cases I'm sure that there are no words yet created on earth to possibly give them true justice. Yet I endeavour, nevertheless.

Second, I'm sure you are going to find some of these amazing experiences very difficult to believe. You must understand that what I share with you is *not* fictional; it is true in every detail. I know it, because I lived it. What I share with you is not something I read about in a book, it's something I physically, spiritually, and supernaturally experienced.

No doctor, psychologist, clergyman, or other person, regardless of their learned study, could ever convince me that what I experienced was anything other than what I am about to tell you it was. All this preamble is to say that I, a totally sane man, have been "there and back"—and therefore I will object to anyone who disputes or suggests that they know more, unless they have been "there and back" themselves.

It is my utmost hope and full intention that the accounts I'm about to share with you will give you new hope, and help you better to understand and believe how you, too, can overcome many of the obstacles in life that stand in your way. Also included are those obstacles that may be standing in the way of a loved one—and that is *regardless the size or the nature* of those obstacles.

I'm convinced that anyone who truly endeavours and properly utilizes what I am about to share will be able to tap into an almost inconceivable resource that few on earth even realize exists.

CHAPTER TWO

The First Attack

For thirty years, the severity and nature of my periodic episodes of mental torment were, for the most part, a personal secret. Given the bizarre nature of these horrific attacks, I chose not to tell my foster parents or, later in life, my superiors or doctors. This was primarily because I couldn't trust what their conclusion may have been; and that was probably part and parcel of my inability to explain it or understand it fully myself, at the time. Nor did I ever hear of any medical explanation, aside from these symptoms possibly being tell-tale signs of insanity—which is what I feared they might diagnose it as. I also chose not to tell my wife until later in marriage, because by the time I got married, I felt I had it hidden well enough and I was learning how to live with it; so I didn't want to scare her unnecessarily. I knew one thing for certain: I was *not* insane, and I didn't deserve that diagnosis. So I kept these struggles to myself—mostly.

At times, when I did choose to tell a close friend some aspects of what I was going through, it may have been more for the therapy I hoped it afforded me. It seemed to help me mentally, just letting someone else know a snippet of what I was living with. Inadvertently, I think I was also testing the waters as to whether or not my close friend would think I was going crazy, and could thereby act as a gauge for me, as to what others may think if they happened to find out. I can add that, living with and effectively concealing these adverse psychological phenomena over such a long period of time became a way of life for me. In fact, for the longest time I thought that this was as normal as life would ever be. That was until the attacks got much worse—which, thankfully, was just prior to me finding the ultimate, definitive and most wonderful solution.

"The sudden fear factor was enough to scare me to a point of near mental collapse."

Before I go further, I have to once again share that any attempt to describe in words—and hope to have you totally understand—what I actually experienced emotionally and mentally during each of these attacks is, I expect, nearly impossible. I have come to realize, however, that some attempt to share my story will surely be more beneficial than no attempt at all. And so, to assist you, the reader, to understand better the magnitude of my mental attacks, I will add this: *"Should what I describe in words not sound to you as being all that profound, let me assure you now that during every single attack I underwent, the sudden fear factor was enough to scare me to a point of near mental collapse. I can describe it best as torture by means of terror."* I need not say more.

As I write now, near the age of sixty-five—and even though the first encounter was forty-seven years ago—I can remember the time and place and the actual sequence of events as if it were yesterday. The suddenness and jolt of the first attack was a complete surprise. I was eighteen years old, and I still remember it in living detail. The unthinkable was (and little did I know then) that these torments were going to continue now for another thirty years, and become something I would have to continue to hide from others, and cope with the best I could figure out along the way.

Author at age 18
Holy Cross Yearbook

I'M EIGHTEEN

I had to repeat Grade 12 in Manitoba, after failing miserably the year prior at Holy Cross high school in St. Boniface (a suburb of Winnipeg). My foster mother (my second) had decided that I should attend a more structured, Christian high school— one that required a dress code, and where the students experienced a stricter lifestyle. So instead of attending the local high school near the little town of Stratton, Ontario where we lived, Mom found me places to board in Winnipeg, about a four and a half hour drive from home.

Not being able to secure the same accommodation as the year prior, to repeat my Grade 12 I attended St. Norbert High School on the outskirts of Winnipeg. Mom, a very determined woman, God bless her, was able to find me *a* room and board at the Oblate Fathers' Novitiate in St. Norbert. Here I soon made friends with a couple of other guys who were also boarding at the Novitiate for the same reason. In particular, Gilbert, who was from a small town in southern Manitoba and also doing Grade 12, soon became my best friend. Gilbert and I, although strangers before this year, had in common a few other guys who were known and friends to both of us. That made our friendship happen that much quicker.

Our school was within walking distance of the Novitiate, and it was on a beautiful sunny September day just after our walk back from school that my first attack happened. Nothing out of the ordinary had happened earlier that day that could have triggered such an attack. On that particular day however, we had played football after school; during the game I was

Oblate Father's Novitiate, St. Norbert, Manitoba, 1968

accused of elbowing, and had a bit of a verbal and physical confrontation with an opposing player. On the way back to my room following the game, I was physically exhausted as well as emotionally and mentally fatigued by the confrontation. Our rooms were on the third floor of the Novitiate; Gilbert's room was at one end of the corridor and my room at the far other end. When I arrived at my room, it was warm; the sun filled my room, the bed was inviting and I decided to lie down to rest for a bit before supper.

I didn't recognize the physical signs—what started to happen to me after a few minutes of lying down—as anything alarming. In the years that followed, however, I certainly would recognize them as dangerous, and fight them with every ounce of my energy. But this day, I didn't know of the danger, and I simply enjoyed the warmth of the sunlight and the comfort of my bed; I was facing the window as I began to relax completely. But then my body started to do something very different. It started to "tingle"—much like when blood starts to rush back into your body after the circulation was cut off from a part of it.

> *"Unknowingly, I lost normal consciousness... and was propelled into another, new conscious state..."*

I was exhausted, and the tingling sensation was very inviting; so I just allowed it to envelop me from head to toe. Unknowingly, I lost normal consciousness within seconds, and was propelled into another, new conscious state—one that was much more real, and much more *alive* than what we normally experience. No one could ever suggest to me that I was simply asleep and dreaming, because after thirty years of enduring these symptoms I can recognize fully the major differences between going to sleep with common dreams, and dealing with the supernatural. It's as easy for me to distinguish as it is to distinguish night from day. Going though this trance-like physical and mental transition—or passage into another state—isn't what anyone experiences when going to sleep. There's no question about this.

TRAPPED

In my new conscious state, I was still lying down on my bed enjoying the sunlight, just like a few moments before. I felt much more relaxed now and was totally overwhelmed by how peaceful I was. I wasn't at all aware that I had changed consciousness; in other words, my mind had totally forgotten about the *tingling*, and that a transition had even taken place; but I did remember that I had just lain down to rest before supper. I lay in bed, feeling absolute peace and tranquility—and yet dangerously ignorant of the fact that my body was now immobilized and totally out of the control of my earthly will or consciousness. I don't think this tranquility and peace, and the feeling of being more alive, more real than in human consciousness, can be understood by anyone who has never made that transition. Nothing was ever so wonderful as what I was now feeling. Nor did I recognize it as being out of the ordinary; I simply soaked in it, because it was so peaceful and relaxing.

> *"Instantly, the absolute peace and tranquility I had been experiencing changed to horror."*

And then, suddenly that beautiful warm and inviting sun actually started to move towards my window; I started to gasp, wondering what was happening. *How on earth could that happen? My God, it's moving!*

Instantly, the absolute peace and tranquility I had been experiencing changed to horror and terror, as the sun started to hurtle towards my window. I needed to get up immediately and warn Gilbert! It was only then I realized that my body was as if it was frozen: my spirit, my conscious mind, was trapped inside this heavily weighted corpse that refused to move! What was happening? It became dark, and I suddenly felt claustrophobic. I was frantic. My spirit was trapped, and I *had* to regain normal consciousness. But how? This evil, dark place was unimaginable; my spirit screamed, trying to connect to my body and my mind. But with my body lying as if dead on the bed, that seemed impossible.

Fear and terror gave me strength, and with it I focused every ounce of energy to have my spirit start moving some part of my body; so I decided to try to move one of my little fingers. Screaming while I focused my every thought and energy, and after what seemed like minutes, I finally got one little finger on my corpse to move; the little finger on my right hand finally moved, ever so slightly. Then, incredibly—and it seemed almost instantaneous—I could feel the rush of life coming into the rest of my physical body. It was like a massive infilling of blood being poured back in everywhere, all at once in one big flood. My spirit now struggled and fought desperately to regain normal consciousness; my mind fought hard to re-enter and start working again with my brain; and then, after near-total exhaustion and concentration, my mind broke in and made the connection with my brain; my eyes opened wide; my normal consciousness awakened. I gasped for a huge breath of air. I was breathing again, and I leapt out of bed utterly petrified. Totally exhausted, I thanked God it was over—whatever in hell that was!

> *"Frightened nearly to death, and perplexed beyond measure, I had new reason to run."*

Frightened nearly to death, and perplexed beyond measure, I had new reason to run as fast as I could down the corridor to tell Gilbert about what had happened. I ran so fast in fact that I couldn't stop in time, and my fist went through the gyprock wall at the other end of the hall. How would I explain that hole in the wall to the Oblate priests? Thinking back, I can't imagine that I could have explained what had just happened to me very well to Gilbert, either; in my excited state, I must have sounded like some kind of a nut-case, because even I didn't know what had really happened. Nevertheless, Gilbert—being a good friend—comforted me to some extent, even though he couldn't possibly have understood the severity and complexity of what I was trying to explain to him.

What in hell's creation had happened to me? And more important, what could have caused this to happen? A key feature that I'd later come to recognize as part of the pattern—and that added immensely to the horrific shock effect—was that I was first allowed to feel so much at peace, just prior to being confronted by the sudden horror. This going from total tranquility to instantaneous horror would become the pattern for every episode to come.

CHAPTER THREE

The Cause

I was hiding with my two younger brothers at the edge of a forested area beyond a field behind our farmhouse. I was six years old. I looked through the branches down the hill across the field at our house below. Our mother and many of my older brothers and sisters, who were scattered near by, were hiding with us.

We were a family of five boys and five girls. My older sisters were telling us younger boys to keep quiet. It didn't make sense to me why we had to be quiet; and it seemed like some kind of game. We hadn't been told from whom we were hiding. We younger boys huddled together behind a bush and just giggled.

As we hid and tried to remain quiet, I recall my father coming into the field, walking up the hill. He now stood near the edge of the forest, just below where we were hiding. My brothers, sisters and Mom crouched low behind bushes so as not to be seen. My Dad looked back and forth, but couldn't see anyone. Then he called out, to see if anyone would answer. "Shhhh," we could hear from our sisters; so no one answered. Dad then called my name and that of my two younger brothers: *"Jimmy, Michael, George, there's some candy for you on the table down at the house!"* he said in a loud voice. Not knowing the importance of staying hidden, Dad's trick to find everyone worked on us younger boys. I immediately rushed out of the bush, past Dad and ran down the hill towards the house. My two younger brothers were running not far behind me. My legs being a year older than theirs, I arrived at the house a minute or so before my brothers. That was just enough time to find the three bags of candy on the table, just as Dad had promised. I promptly hid one entire bag in my pocket for myself, and then told my brothers after they arrived that there were only two bags of candy and we had to split them three ways. They agreed.

Soon, everyone else returned from the forest; the house was busy again and the hiding game was over. It was only many years later that I came to understand that it was my father that we had been hiding from. Why, on that particular day, was Mom so afraid of Dad that we had to hide? It was never made clear to me.

AN ACCIDENT

My two younger brothers and I loved being allowed to get into the back of our pickup truck and go down the hill to the LaVallee corner store. It was on one such day that I learned a new word. There was all kinds of talk around our house that an "*accident*" had happened down at the LaVallee corner store; hmm, what did that mean? The excitement in everyone's voices had me wanting to know just what an *accident* was. I was very glad to be allowed to ride in the back of the pickup as we all jumped into the back of the truck to go down the hill to see the accident. Wow! Today I was going to find out what that word "accident" meant!

As our truck slowed down near the store, I saw a number of bright red flares burning on the side of the road, some red flags, and some people moving about. Nobody seemed happy or excited, and everyone in our truck was pretty quiet now. There wasn't much more to see, and unbeknownst to me, they had already removed the vehicles that were involved; so an "accident,"

I then concluded, simply had to do with something sad. As we drove away and headed back up the hill, no one told me any different; so that became my understanding for the word "accident." Thinking back now, however, that little event was a foreshadowing of a major *"incident"* that was soon going to happen on our farm.

FARM TIDBITS

Our farm did have some animals; I remember chickens, pigs, horses and dogs. I was alone with Dad one day in the chicken coop and he showed me how to take a fresh egg from under a hen, crack it open with one hand and swallow all the contents in one gulp. I don't recall ever trying it myself, but he was very good at it.

One of my older brothers apparently put a saddle on our big pig to go for a ride. There was a lot of talk about this later in the kitchen, among my brothers and sisters; it had something to do with either the pig dying or a steer dying because of riding it too much. I think they were all scared Dad was going to find out why the animal died.

Author's Dad on the farm

The barn was big, and sometimes it had lots of hay in the hayloft. Playing up there, swinging from a rope, was total fun. I sat one day outside the barn and watched my Dad take all these newborn puppies one by one out of a gunnysack. He held them each in turn by the tail, and smashed their little heads up against the corner of the barn; then he threw them on the ground, and they landed beside me. The mother dog was pacing back and forth whining, and she sounded very sad as she sniffed the dead little bodies. I was also very sad. I didn't understand why all the little dogs had to die; they were so much fun to play with.

A similar event happened some time later. Someone was playing on the big tractor that was parked in the barnyard, and caused it to roll back a few feet. It wasn't running at the time, but it started to move; and the big wheel of the tractor rolled right on top of a puppy. The puppy was golden brown, his head and half his body that was sticking out looked fine, the other half was under the big wheel. The pup didn't move any more. I went into the house and I tried to tell my brothers and sisters about how the puppy needed help, but an entire day went by and nobody bothered to move the tractor off the puppy. I went out the next day to see the mother dog still lying beside the tractor with her nose right beside the dead puppy, there were ants all over the puppy's head. I sat there with her for a while; the sound coming out of her was very sad, and it made me sad that no one came to help move the tractor off the puppy.

One day, my Dad was out in the barnyard and was having quite a time with a very big pig. He finally managed to put a gunnysack over the head of the pig, and at that point the pig seemed to quiet down some. Suddenly, Dad took an axe and swung it as hard as he could and hit the pig somewhere on the head with the back of the axe. The pig kicked and squealed something terrible. The loudness of the squealing and all the shouting that was going on was very upsetting, and certainly scary. Someone shouted about the need to stab the pig in the throat, and that made me run away. Later that night, a nice warm bonfire was burning outside, and many of the family were having a great time around the fire. They were roasting some of the pig, and I tried tasting the roasted pig's tail. It was very good and my younger brothers and I fought over having a turn with the roasted pig's tail.

DÉJÀ VU

Just prior to me writing these next few paragraphs, I got up from my computer to take a short break. I poured a glass of water, and as a coincidence (or God-incident) would have it, I decided to make some popcorn. I shared half with my wife and went back to writing. Then, as I sat with my glass of water and the smell of popcorn in my office, an eerie sense of déjà vu came over me. Then I realized which recollection I was ready to write about. I sat back in my chair for a moment to collect my thoughts, and I was somewhat amazed at the timing of wanting to have popcorn. In the room with me now was that desire for popcorn that I had experienced, waiting in the kitchen one evening long ago: November, 1956.

THAT NOVEMBER NIGHT

I was six years and three months old at the time. On our farm that night there was much activity in our kitchen. Dad wasn't home, and my aunt, my Mom and a lot of my older brothers and sisters were busy in the kitchen. Some of them were sitting around the kitchen table, playing cards. It was getting late, but I was being allowed to watch for a little while longer before going to bed. Leaning against the table, I was just tall enough so that I could watch what was going on. On the other side of the table directly across from me was the kitchen stove. Mom was standing at the stove with her back to me. She was making popcorn and I couldn't wait to get some. Off to the right of the stove was the open door to the pantry. What no one knew at the time, and what everyone came to understand later, was that our Dad was lurking in the dark outside and looking in through that pantry window. In his hand he had a loaded high-powered rifle and a pocket full of bullets. The excite-

Author at age 6

ment and fun, the popcorn and laughter that our family was having in the kitchen was about to have a sudden and traumatic change; terror was about to unfold.

> *"My legs went completely numb, I couldn't breathe, and fear paralyzed my body."*

Everyone in the kitchen must have heard the sound of the breaking glass. I certainly did; it came from the pantry and it sounded like the window. Mom, who was tending to the popcorn on the stove, leaned over a bit to see what it might be; as I was watching Mom do this, the terrifying blast of the first shot hit Mom in the head and she fell to the left. Stunned by the horror of what I saw and the ear-deafening explosion of the gun, my legs went completely numb, I couldn't breathe, and fear paralyzed my body. My legs actually collapsed from under me. They had no feeling left in them, none whatsoever; and I dropped to the floor under the table, unable to move. Mom fell near the doorway that led out of the kitchen to the living room and the upstairs bedrooms. I was numb with fear and frozen; I couldn't move, and from under the table, I could see Mom lying on the floor. Then, amidst the confusion of the family screaming, hollering, running, there was blood; and then there was another horrific blast of the gun. I tried to cover my ears and close my eyes.

Hidden from the others under the kitchen table in the dark, I was still unable to move. I opened my eyes again and could see some of the adults on the floor around Mom, frantically trying to help her. As I was just lying there and watching the confusion, I was suddenly grabbed from behind by someone and picked up. I was quickly carried over past Mom to get out of the kitchen, and taken upstairs. The bedroom was very dark. Some of my brothers and sisters were already up there, and I was now on the bed, not sure what to do. It was so dark! One of my brothers or sisters, I know, was hiding under the bed; I could hear him or her moving around under there. Some were on the floor of the bedroom praying, *"Our Father, who art in heaven...."* Another was crying over and over, *"Oh my God! Oh my God! Oh my God!"*

Much of the confusion had moved from the kitchen to the very dark bedroom upstairs. I could still hear some low screaming and praying going on; and it seemed like almost

Author's mother—Mary Hnatiuk, killed when only 39 years old

everyone was crying somewhere in the dark. A short time later, I heard another gunshot outside, a little further away. I laid down on the bed and didn't dare move. Finally, I became so very tired I fell asleep. Later, I was awakened and remember having to leave the house in the dark.

That night Mom and Dad died and the rest of my family survived.

Mary Hnatiuk, 1917—1956
Fort Frances Cemetery

Peter Hnatiuk, 1902—1956
Fort Frances Cemetery

I later came to understand that after missing the subject of his second shot, for whatever reason my Dad went out to the barnyard and shot himself.

CHAPTER FOUR

Torments

FOURTEEN YEARS LATER

It was an absolutely beautiful summer day for a walk; the sun was shining, and its warmth was so welcoming. There was a gentle breeze in the air, and the slow-moving brook on the other side of the street, just off to my left, made my walk feel heavenly perfect.

"I was really taken by her appearance... and by how stunningly beautiful she appeared."

As I made my way along the sidewalk, I was full of anticipation—excited, feeling so alive; and today, I couldn't wait to get to my destination. Because of the quickened pace I was walking at, I could see that I would soon overtake the young girl a few yards ahead of me. I guessed she would be about sixteen years old; she had long blonde hair, and was walking in the same direction as I was. As I drew closer, I was really taken by her appearance; by her hair that gently blew with the breeze and brushed over her shoulders; and by how stunningly beautiful she appeared, even though up to this point, I could only see her back. As I drew near, my full concentration was focused on this young lady. I couldn't wait to pass her, just to say "Hello." She appeared so happy! I caught a whisper of her perfume—and just as I was about to pass her, she turned around.

Suddenly and abruptly she turned around to confront me. Her face was that of a ferocious demon-like animal! It was huge, dark and ugly—satanic, right out of the depths of hell.

"Its horrid growl could only have come from the depths of hell itself."

It attacked me, as would a lion leaping toward you. Its mouth opened, and its long horrid tongue lashed out directly at my face. The smell was putrid. Its eyes were glaring and full of blood, and its horrid growl could only have come from the depths of hell itself.

I instantly went into shock. My legs went numb. I couldn't breathe, and fear rushed though my body from head to foot. Stunned with fear and totally paralyzed, I collapsed. And as I fell, everything turned dark. My spirit instantly realized that it was once again trapped inside my dark, heavy, lifeless corpse. I was alone in there, trapped in the dark with that beast.

Again my spirit screamed, trying to connect to my normal consciousness; and again I went through the excruciating mental pain of focusing every ounce of energy to try to start moving just one of my little fingers. *Why, why would my body not respond?* I was frantic. Then, after what seemed like an eternity, and with every ounce of energy focused on one little finger, the tip of it moved ever so little—and that somehow triggered an instantaneous rush of life that exploded through my body, and what felt like blood pouring back in everywhere.

The transition out of that state was both physically and mentally painful, and I was only somewhat relieved when I knew that the transition out of it had actually started. One last step: my spirit had to immediately fight now to regain normal consciousness; and again, after nearly total exhaustion and concentration, my spirit finally connected again to my physical brain, and my eyes suddenly opened wide.

> *"I gasped for air and started breathing again."*

Yes! I gasped for air and started breathing again; my normal consciousness was restored, my brain was again in control of my body; my body was responding, and I leapt up off the couch from where I had lain down to rest only minutes earlier. Thank God it was over!

After every one of these out-of-body hallucinogenic-type attacks, I was physically and mentally exhausted. I wouldn't dare lie down again for the longest time, for fear of being taken control of yet again by that *other* supernatural force that could only be described as demonic. How could something that had the capacity and power of taking my spirit to such an overwhelmingly alive and beautiful place be so evil and destructive? Time after time, it was so deceptive; and time after time, I was subjected to a new ugly and gut-wrenching torment.

These types of attacks, and many other horrid variations, continued for years. Some seasons were worse than others; the attacks ranged from as few as two or three per month to as many as two to three per week. It frustrated me most that every time, I could be so totally and completely deceived, trapped, and then helplessly led to the slaughter. Each time, I was totally unaware that a transition of consciousness had even taken place, and that I was being set up, yet again, to be instantaneously traumatized.

Again and again, my spirit was taken to a place of absolute peace and joy; and I always felt so *much more alive and real* than normal, earthly consciousness; and then each time, I would suffer instantaneous and unimaginable horror and shock. The evil force always ensured that it first took me to a place of heightened beauty—which was calm, peaceful and heavenly—before it would then suddenly throw me instantly into what could only be described as the pits of hell. It was like this evil thing wanted my mind to be destroyed, and through these repeated torments it was going to make that happen. What was so disappointing to me was the deception; once the *tinglings* consumed me, it had the ability to totally deceive me every time. It had the ability to erase my memory of all the earlier torments just long enough to trap me into another— it had to be laughing when it successfully shocked all life right out of me one more time.

> "My out-of-body consciousness had a much greater and much higher level of realism."

The greatest mystery, and what was so perplexing, was that this other conscious state was so much more real, more alive than my normal everyday consciousness. My out-of-body consciousness had a much greater and much higher level of realism; one that doesn't have the burden we experience when our spirit is contained within a human body. In comparing the two, I realized that in my normal (earthly) conscious state, my spirit feels the additional heaviness of having to control my physical body. This led me to believe that during these episodes, somehow my spirit had to be leaving my body; and hence the reason it was so difficult for my spirit to regain control of my body (which then acted like a corpse) when all hell broke loose. When I was being tormented, I immediately sought refuge by trying to get back into the corpse I had been stolen from, and/or deceived into earlier abandoning.

What had to concern me most was to know that whatever had the power to cause all of this to happen was also very evil; and so disturbingly destructive.

> "Whatever had the power to cause all of this to happen was also very evil."

I started to analyze this phenomenon, and concluded that this other *something* could only want one thing—and that was to systematically destroy me mentally; and that it was relentless in pursuing this task. I was alone in an ongoing war to keep my sanity, and this unknown enemy had the advantage of me never knowing when I was going to be attacked next. Who could I possibly trust, or make understand what was going on with me in these supernatural encounters, without the possibility of being misdiagnosed as insane? No one.

Continual self-analysis on my part, however, did discover something important…a pattern did exist, and I found out that there were certain conditions that seemed to cause the attacks to increase.

I NEED HELP

After so many attacks over so many years, I had come to realize that the timing and the success of the attacks depended largely on the strength of my physical and mental condition just prior to me lying down.

> "This other force would only attempt to **envelop** (consume and overtake) me when I was either physically or mentally fatigued."

It became apparent that this other force would only attempt to *envelop* (consume and overtake) me when I was either physically or mentally fatigued; and it was successful almost every time that both those conditions came together. In other words, I was most vulnerable when I was weakest, and the only warning sign I was given was the *tingling* sensation that would start to happen a few seconds before consumption.

Once the *tingling* started to enter my body, I sometimes wouldn't have the physical or mental strength left in me to stop it from consuming me. When I realized the *tingling* was starting to happen, I only had seconds to decide to fight—or give up and let it consume me. Sometimes I could fight to muster just enough willpower and energy to sit back up; but those efforts were very exhausting. I cannot emphasize enough how the internal mental struggle to regain total control of my body and my mind once the *tingling* process had started was gut-wrenchingly difficult and exhausting. When I was successful in interceding (interrupting the process), I'd bounce up and refuse to lie down until I was practically dead tired. Often I tried reading a book; sometimes I'd go for a walk; but eventually I'd collapse on my bed or sofa and then accept whatever happened.

Another horrible aspect of the *tingling* sensations was that they were very deceptive. The *tingling* sensations would deceive me into believing I was being invited to a place of rest, much like when you are peacefully drifting off for a nap on your sofa.

> *"The **tingling** acted like a fatal attraction, and I was always drawn to succumb to it."*

It's so inviting and restful! All this would be coupled with the fact that my body so desperately wanted rest; so succumbing to the *tingling* would be almost automatic. That deception was difficult to recognize; and often when I did realize what was happening, I couldn't fight against it because I was simply far too tired, and I needed rest. The *tingling* acted like a fatal attraction, and I was always drawn to succumb to it. When I desperately needed the most rest, the *tingling* invitation would almost certainly come shortly after lying down. I grew to recognize the attraction as a deception, and had to force myself each time to resist it; a tug-of-war that in itself became a form of mental torture. Each time, I only had a few seconds to make up my mind—do I succumb and relax and soon be terrified, or fight to survive regardless my fatigue?

"Another incredible phenomenon started to happen only a month after we were married."

After my marriage to Ellen in September 1973, another incredible phenomenon started to happen only a month after we were married. I found that during normal consciousness, I started suffering from a fear of wanting to hurt my wife. This was sickening, and I couldn't believe it was happening to me! What in hell was going on? Why couldn't I have a normal life? In the back of my mind, I was being reminded of what my father had done to our family; and if whatever defeated my father mentally had that much power, did I now have to live with the fear that it might eventually defeat me?

As it turned out, this new phobia took on a life of its own; and unexpectedly, it manifested during my navy career as deep chest pains. Not knowing what was going on with these sudden sharp pains in my chest, I visited the military doctors on at least two occasions complaining about what I was experiencing. Both times, I was assured that I had a

Author's marriage to Ellen, September 8th, 1973.

very healthy heart (as a man in his twenties should have), and they could find no problems with me physically. I felt they were surely missing something, because these sudden pains were enough to knock me to my knees.

Therefore, unconvinced by their diagnosis and not wanting to arouse suspicion, I bought some medical books and started to research the problem myself. After extensive reading, I happened upon what I believed was the source of my chest pain. This fear of hurting my wife, I self diagnosed as having a form of what today is called *obsessive-compulsive disorder* (OCD), which I

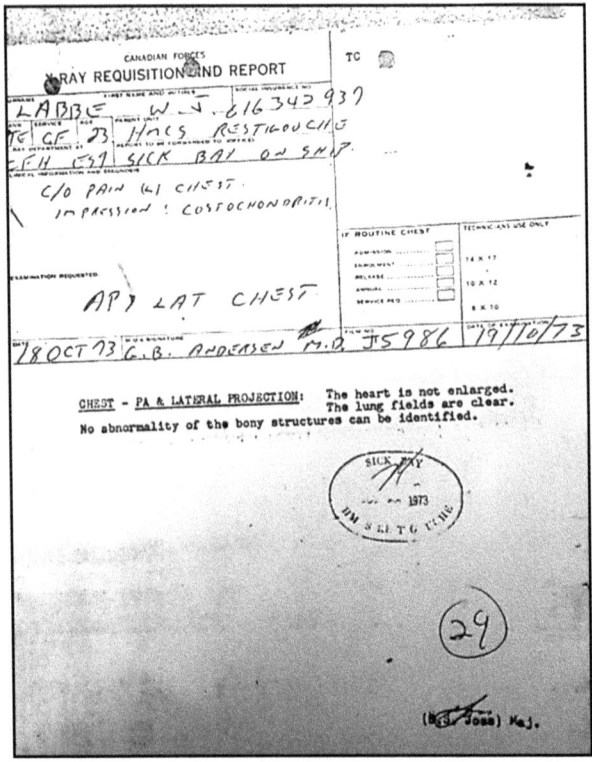

Author's medical record of his complaint of severe chest pains on October 19th, 1973. Author's name was still under his adopted name of Wilfred J. Labbe.

found out can at times also manifest as deep physical chest pains. I didn't like any of it, but at least now I felt I understood the pain. Making the connection also helped alleviate some of the fear factor, which in turn reduced the episodes of pain.

With my new family, the *tingling*, the torments, the mental attacks on each occasion now intensified to new levels, with new deceptions and horror. The question still hung heavily over me: what was this mental torment I was fighting against, anyway? I concluded that a person's own sane mind doesn't plot to destroy itself; and secondly, this was far too real to be a fabrication of my mind. It was obvious to me that my issue was separate from my physical brain, because while I was being tormented, my physical body was lying as if dead on the bed or sofa—I wasn't even connected to it.

> "I concluded that a person's own sane mind doesn't plot to destroy itself..."

So my logical conclusion after all these years of torment became that *this was not something happening with my mind* (my physical brain) but rather *someone who was tampering with my spirit.* Not being able to put my finger on it, I concluded that it came from somewhere within that other conscious state—somewhere my spirit was being taken; and wherever in hell that was, it was certainly in another dimension—and one more real to life than normal consciousness.

It was after ten years of this type of on-again, off-again shock treatment, and just as if this thing could read my mind, as if it knew I was starting to figure it out, *it spoke to me....*

This horrific event happened when I was trapped in the middle of yet another one of those mental tortures. I was at the point where I had just been shocked and traumatized beyond belief, and was now totally paralyzed by fear. It was dark—pitch black. I was totally vulnerable and at its mercy. It was just before I would start to fight to get my body (my corpse) to move that I heard its horrid voice right behind me. At that moment, I could feel the hairs on the back of my neck rising up. I was instantly taken to a new and higher level of fear—one I couldn't ever have dreamt possible. Its gut-wrenching, deep, vile and powerfully evil voice was practically breathing down my neck.

> *"Its gut-wrenching, deep, vile and powerfully evil voice was practically breathing down my neck."*

It was so dark! My stricken mind felt it should have exploded from fear…the battle then ensued to escape, and I had to focus to get my corpse moving again. Again after tremendous effort, and through the process I had come to know so very well, I was able to escape.

I couldn't believe what I had just experienced! As days passed, I realized that the fear of hearing the voice of that *thing*, that *someone*—that fear had now followed me into my normal state. I knew now that I had to tell someone about this, but whom? Who could I tell this secret to, that may be able to help me and not turn me in as some kind of a nut case? Who would possibly understand this bizarre phenomenon—let alone believe that I had heard what could only have been a demon?

I decided for good reason that the person I had to speak to would have to be my best friend's Mom. Yes, Gord's mother, who lived in Vancouver, was the most logical choice. There was something about Gord's Mom that was very different from most other folks. I had only met her on a few

Mrs. MacNeil, Gord's Mom

occasions, but I sensed that something in her was very genuine; and I could tell that she had a confidence in knowing
what she believed in to be very true. I didn't know her all that
well; but I knew her well enough to know that. So yes, it would
be Gord's Mom. But there was one big problem.

I had a real sense that the *thing* that was tormenting me
was actually semi-dormant inside of me, even during my
normal consciousness. Therefore, I figured it would run
deceptive interference to see that I could never meet the one
person who could identify it.

> "It was ingenious at deceiving me, so I decided I had to come up with a better counter-deception."

As crazy as it sounds, I suspected
that the *thing* already had some kind of
power over me and was able at times to
manipulate my thought processes
during my everyday activities. It was
ingenious at deceiving me, so I decided
I had to come up with a better counter-
deception before the *thing* realized what
I was up to. I knew that if I had my friend Gord set up a meeting
for me with his Mom; the *thing* in me would have me make
excuses not to show up for the meeting when the time came. My
mind had become a battlefield, and I had now come to know that;
and it was a battle I knew I couldn't afford to lose.

So to second-guess this *thing*, I came up with a plan to fool
myself into a meeting with Gord's Mom. It was like I had to outsmart this force that was influencing my mind. In other words, if
I didn't know the meeting was going to take place, and I was surprised into the meeting, I wouldn't have any other choice but to
participate. So, when I figured this other thing was dormant in
me, in the greatest of confidence I explained to Gord that my
mental torments had increased to levels I could no longer deal
with. I told him that I had heard a demon speak to me, and I

needed desperately to speak to his mother about it. I explained to Gord that if I knew the meeting was to take place, this other *thing* in my head would never agree to meeting with his Mom, that it would cause me make excuses not to attend, so I needed him to promise to set up a meeting, and in some way fool me into it. I also told him to tell his mother what the subject matter would be. It was important his mother knew it was about a demon talking to me; so in that way, once I was fooled into the meeting with her, I couldn't make up stories that I wanted to meet with her about something else. She would know the subject matter of the meeting, and I'd be trapped into telling her about what had happened. I told Gord to be very careful, because I would now have a paranoia that he was trying to set me up with this meeting and I'd avoid this meeting at all costs.

> *"To explain how I had to outsmart my own mind can only sound bizarre."*

This may all sound very bizarre. That's because it *is* bizarre: my mind had become a battlefield, and to explain how I had to outsmart my own mind can only sound bizarre, so bear with me a bit here. I can assure you it was very necessary for me to plan like this. Something else or someone else had some limited and periodic control over my mind and my body, so I concluded that I had to try and outsmart it, whatever it was.

I pleaded with Gord to make sure he would do this, and he promised me he would see this happen.

CHAPTER FIVE

Post Murder and Suicide

1956

After the murder and suicide of Mom and Dad, I remember Christmas that year—which was only a few weeks after that horrific evening. We were back in the farmhouse; our older brothers and sisters had us three younger boys looking into the Christmas catalogue. I was delighted to be told that I could have any toy I wanted! It was so hard to decide; but I finally picked out a garage set. Then, on or about Christmas Day, some men (Shriners) showed up at our home; they wore funny tall red hats that had some black laces hanging off to one side. There were quite a few of these men. They played with us, laughed and made jokes. We had a lot of fun that day. One man with that funny hat played with me and with my new garage set.

On the farm, not too long afterward, I remember having to talk to a woman and a man I had never seen before; they wanted to talk to me. Not long after, my younger brother Michael and I were dressed up, put in a car with them and we drove away from the farm. Some in our family said "goodbye" to Michael and me that day; but we didn't really understand why, or for how long we were going to be gone. I found this strange, because as days and weeks went by, I didn't understand why we couldn't be with our other brothers and sisters, back on the farm. Unknown to us, an adoption had taken place....

"Unknown to us, an adoption had taken place."

With this new man and woman, Michael and I ended up in a town we did not know, called Atikokan. The man's name was Bill and the woman was called Ann. They both treated us pretty nice at first; but Ann soon let us know that there were a lot of rules we had to follow. She kept telling people she knew that "Bill always wanted two boys," but that she only wanted one. After a few weeks, they said it was OK for us to call them Mom and Dad. We found that sort of strange, but we tried our best. A bigger surprise came when they told us we had new names: I was told my name was no longer Jim Hnatiuk, but now it would be Wilfred Labbe. "Wilfred"—yuck! I didn't like that name much; and neither did Michael like his new name. When "Mom" wasn't around, Michael and I still used our real names with each other, and we'd have a good laugh about the silly ones they had given us. After all, we figured that when we saw our brothers and sisters again, they'd still be calling us by our real names; so it made sense to us that we keep them.

This new mom made all the rules, and was always strict—especially when "Dad" wasn't around; our new dad was always really nice, but he was gone far too often.

Our new mom and dad had two good friends; we were told to call them "uncle" and "auntie." Uncle and auntie had a daughter named Beverly, who was about two years older than me. She would continually boss Michael and me around, and tell us what to do; and if we didn't do it, she would tell our new mom that we had done something bad. Our mom always believed Beverly and not Michael or me. One day Beverly told "mom" that I had said a swear word. As a result, I had to spend a long time in a small room, being lectured by this new mom. Over and over again she wanted me to admit to having said the bad word. I really could not remember saying it, and I explained that what I had said could only have sounded like that swear word. "Mom" didn't believe me, and was very angry. She took away some money "Dad" had given me before he left, and she put soap in my mouth. I think Beverly just made up the lie to punish me. I wished Dad had been home.

THE TABLE TURNS

Often the two families would go camping, Michael and I totally enjoyed camping, and most times the two families had small camping trailers to stay in. On one camping trip, my mom and Beverly's mom were making a big fuss about Beverly, because she was crying uncontrollably after being stung on the arm by a hornet. It seemed very strange when mom and auntie came to my brother Michael and asked him if he had to pee. We really didn't understand why; so Michael, being sort of scared, said no, he couldn't pee right now. So mom spun around quickly and asked me if I had to pee—she said it was very important that I try. I said, "OK, I might be able to go." I said this with absolutely no idea what was going to happen next. At that, we all went off behind the trailer into a wooded area. They then told Beverly, who was crying because of the hornet sting, to turn her head and not look. I was then told to take down my pants and pee on her arm over the hornet bite. I was absolutely delighted by this great news and I suddenly realized that I was going to do everything I could to see that I did. Yahoo! Yes, I was successful and delighted to be peeing all over Beverly's arm. Michael was told to leave and not to look; but I knew he did—I could see him giggling a little way off, hiding behind a tree. Later that night, Michael and I had some good laughs and talked about it under the covers until we fell asleep. Michael had wished he had known why "Mom" was asking him to pee, because he said he would have tried really hard—especially after finding out he was going to pee on Beverly.

A few days later, Beverly took Michael and me aside, and demanded that we never *ever* tell her girl friends or a living soul what had happened. We giggled, and then agreed we wouldn't tell; but we also told her that our silence came with conditions. From that day forward, Beverly treated Michael and me a lot better. We actually became the best of friends, and Beverly often defended us, even from "Mom." Michael and I, on the other hand, kept our promise never to tell her girl friends or anyone else what had happened. (Hmmm. I just broke that promise!)

One Sunday morning, we were at St. Patrick's church. During the service—and to our absolute delight—Michael and I spotted our younger brother, George, sitting on the other side of the church. We hadn't seen any of our other brothers and sisters since leaving the farm. Wow, George was right here in church with us! And he also spotted us. We were super excited, and couldn't wait for the service to end in order to see him. Our parents seemed to notice our excitement, and told us to behave. After church was over, we couldn't find George anywhere. We were very sad to realize that he must have left before the service was over. For a long time, Michael and I talked about us seeing George in church; our parents said it might have been someone who only *looked* like George. In bed at night, Michael and I secretly talked about how we knew it was our brother George, and no one could ever change our minds on that. The following Sundays at church, we would always be looking for George again. But he was never there. Soon we left that town.

Later in life I learned that yes, our younger brother George had lived for a time with his new adoptive parents in that same town. Our parents had realized what had happened at church that Sunday, and made sure we didn't connect with him.

We moved now to an area called Theresa Gold Mines near Long Lac in Ontario—a place that was very cold in winter. We lived and traveled in a very small dome-shaped trailer that was all silver on the outside. Dad towed the trailer with his truck. He wasn't around much; sometimes he would be away for weeks before coming home. Mom was very strict, so we always enjoyed when Dad came home. Mom didn't treat us the same when Dad was home; it was more like she pretended to like us when Dad was around. I remember one evening in the little trailer, Dad made popcorn; we put some on a string to put on a tree. Dad also read us books before we went to bed. But all too soon, Dad would go away again.

Later in life, I found out that Dad (William "Bill" Labbe) worked on heavy equipment in the mines, and we had traveled from one mining community to another in this little trailer that was our home.

> *"Mom was very strict; I don't think she really wanted us."*

Mom was very strict; I don't think she really wanted us. She was always making new rules. She always told us that we should behave like another family she knew. This other family apparently had children who were so good, and we were apparently always so bad. Why couldn't we be like the children in this other family? Over and over again, we'd hear about this other family and how good their children were. I'm not even sure this other family existed, because Michael and I never did meet them.

For one of my punishments, Mom would give me only cheese sandwiches in my lunch for school for an entire week. She knew that I hated cheese, so that was my punishment. What she didn't seem to realize is that Michael loved cheese. Michael and I would always take care of each other, so he would trade me his peanut butter sandwiches for my cheese sandwiches; and we felt good knowing that Mom didn't know the difference.

It would take me some thirty years to develop a taste for even a mild cheddar cheese—which I do enjoy today.

There was one other food I could not eat, and that was mushroom soup. Once, we were visiting at someone else's home, and I had to sit over a bowl of mushroom soup for least an hour or more. I was told I was to eat it "or else"—and Mom meant it! Another adult in the house tried to convince Mom to give me something else to eat. Mom said, "Absolutely not!" I finally realized that I would never be able to get out of the chair unless I did eat it. So reluctantly I tried; I got half the bowl down before vomiting back into the bowl, and some onto the floor. The other adult got angry with my Mom and told her to leave me alone.

I still cannot eat mushroom soup to this day.

CHAPTER SIX

Ojibwa

Later, Michael and I moved in with our new grandparents, who lived right near the town of Long Lac, in northern Ontario. Mom had many brothers (I think five) and they all lived very close to our grandparents' small, blue house on the Ojibwa reserve. Mom's dad (our new Grandpa) was a skinny old white man who spent a lot of time in a rocking chair. Mom's mother, on the other hand, was a very huge Indian woman; and all Mom's brothers (my new uncles) were Indian also.

I certainly remember that first day that we met our new grandmother and stayed at her house. The fact that our new family was Indian didn't bother us at all. What amazed Michael and me was how big Grandma was, and how little and skinny our new white grandfather was. We secretly had a little giggle about what that probably looked like in bed. As luck would have it, I was soon going to find out, because on the first night we met them, I was shocked to find out that until our bedroom was ready, I would be sleeping with my new grandmother in her bed. Being as how she was so big, I couldn't see how that would even be possible.

> *"The fact that our new family was Indian didn't bother us at all."*

The time to go to bed obviously came far too soon. Her room was small, and so was the bed. *"My God,"* I thought, *"How will we both fit on this bed?"* After lying down, I only pretended to go to sleep because I was waiting for Grandma to come to bed. This was a bit frightening; not only did I not know how we were both going to fit, I wasn't even sure if she was going to have clothes on. When she finally came into the bedroom, I made sure I was all the way to the edge of the bed on my side, with my face pointing towards the wall. I didn't dare peek as she was undressing. The wall was painted blue, and the paint was pretty dirty, and I had my nose pushed right up against it. Well, I was sort of amazed, when she plumped herself onto the bed, that we did seem to both fit! I didn't have a lot of room, but I was warm and soon fell asleep. Grandma was already out of bed when I woke up in the morning, and she had a delicious breakfast ready for both Michael and me.

"Our very big grandmother would often make beaver soup."

We both totally loved our new grandmother and her family. Often, Michael and I would go check the beaver traps with our uncles, and that was something we both really enjoyed doing. Our new uncles always spoke nicely to us, and gave us some pretty neat stuff. Our very big grandmother would often make beaver soup, and Michael and I both enjoyed eating it. She also made the best macaroni soup ever! It was amazing how large our grandmother was, and still able to do so much.

Granddad would sit on his rocking chair. Every so often, he would take out a sharp knife and cut off a piece of what looked like a brown bar of soap. He would chew it, and then do a lot of spitting. From time to time, Granddad would tell us why it was good for him to chew that stuff; but Grandma told us not to believe him. Once, when no one was looking, I cut a little piece off for myself and tried it. It felt really good in my mouth, sort of like toffee; but when I swallowed a bit, it tasted just utterly horrible. In fact, I had to vomit and my eyes instantly filled with tears. Michael and I found out later that if we ate a small piece of it with a spoonful of home-made butter, it went down a whole lot better. Sometimes we would wake up in the middle of the night; get up ever so quietly, sneak over by where Granddad kept that brown stuff, and cut a small piece off to eat with butter. Wow! What a treat, if you chewed just a little bit and then swallowed it quickly with that butter! We'd only take very little pieces each time, because we didn't want Granddad to realize some was missing.

A few times, after it got dark outside, I was allowed to go for a ride in the truck with my uncles. When we came near to this big hole in the ground that was filled with everyone's garbage, my uncle would drive very slowly around the hole on this narrow road. He would carefully shine the lights of the truck across the dump, and I would have my nose pushed up against the window to see what it was they were looking for. "There's one!" he said.

"My God!" I sat back in my seat; there was a huge black bear looking right at us, and so very close to the truck! My uncles didn't appear to be alarmed, and then I noticed that the bear was caught by one leg and chained to a tree. The bear was angry, and pulled hard trying to get away. My uncle continued to slowly shine the truck lights to other parts in the dump; and sure enough, he found two other big bears caught by their legs and very angry not being able to get away. As we drove away from the huge hole, my uncles talked about coming back in the morning to shoot all the bears. I was sort of glad they didn't bring me along for that part.

We stayed at our grandparent's place in Long Lac so long that Michael and I started to go to school there. The previous year, we had traveled so much with Dad that we had gone to at least three different schools in three different towns before the year was finished. Michael failed that year, and now had to spend a second year in Grade One. I was now in Grade Three.

> "The language of instruction was entirely French!"

In this little school in Long Lac, everyone was in the same classroom regardless what grade you were in. What really surprised us was that the teacher spoke only in French, and neither Michael nor I knew any French at all. In fact, the language of instruction was entirely French!

After a couple of months, I found that I was able to actually understand a lot of what the teacher was saying. Michael, on the other hand, sat close to me, because he could never figure any of it out, and would always ask me what she was talking about.

On our last day of school for that year, and just before we left to walk down the hill to Grandma's house, I saw the teacher talking to Michael. She seemed to be repeating herself, so I went to find out what the problem might be. I heard her ask Michael (in French) if that was his first year in Grade One, and I was just in time to hear Michael answer "*Oui.*"

Walking down the hill on our way home I asked my brother why he had told the teacher it was his first year in Grade One, when in fact it was his second year. Michael said that he didn't know what she was talking about, so he just guessed and gave her an answer. As a result, the teacher failed Michael again that year; had she known he had already spent two years in Grade One, she would have passed him. He would now have to spend three years in Grade One. I graduated that year to Grade Four.

We liked living with our new grandparents and uncles, and during our time with them we rarely saw Dad or very much of Mom. We missed Dad, but sure didn't miss Mom much.

> *"I never realized that someone could scream and cry for so long."*

It was on a Sunday, and one of those rare occasions where our family was together. Dad was driving us back to Grandma's house in his big car after church on Sunday. I could hear Mom in the front seat; she was concerned, and asking Dad how he was feeling. He said he wasn't feeling very well. They talked a little about Dad having to see a doctor again. After we arrived at our Grandma's place, Dad came beside Michael and me as we walked toward the front door. He stopped us just before going into the house; he rubbed his hands softly over our heads and told us to always remember to be good boys. We told him we would. Dad then walked into the house and fell to the floor with a crash. Mom started screaming. Michael and I were told we had to wait outside. We could hear Mom screaming, asking God over and over why he had taken Dad away from her. Mom cried and screamed for three days and three nights. I never realized that someone could scream and cry for so long. Dad, we found out, had died instantly from a massive heart attack.

After a few days, some men brought Dad's coffin inside the house and put it in Grandma's living room for everyone to look at him. The people prayed, talked and ate food.

Michael and I were told to dress up in our Sunday clothes, so Grandma helped us with that. We were then brought into the room where Dad's coffin was. There were a lot of other people there, most sitting in chairs up against the wall looking at the coffin. It was pretty strange, and everyone went quiet as Michael and I walked into the room all dressed up in our Sunday best.

Mom spoke up and told us that we would never see Dad any more, and that we were to go and kneel on a footstool beside the coffin and pray. Michael and I could see that the coffin was open, and we didn't dare say "No," after having Mom scream and cry for so long. We certainly didn't want *that* to start up again, so we walked across the room towards the coffin.

There was just enough room on the footstool for both Michael and I to kneel together. We were tall enough that our eyes could just see into the coffin and see the dead man in front of us. All dressed up in a suit, it didn't look much like Dad any more. In fact, the body looked pretty eerie.

"Mom's stern green eyes were glaring at me."

Not really sure what we were suppose to be praying, I just faked it with my hands together and my eyes closed. After a few minutes, when Mom figured we were done, she told us that we were to stand on the footstool and lean over into the coffin and kiss Dad on the cheek before leaving. I couldn't believe what I was being told to do, and I certainly didn't want to kiss this dead man that did not look much like Dad. I glanced around to say something, but Mom's stern green eyes were glaring at me, and so were all the people in the room. I knew I had to do it, or else Mom would have a fit. I leaned over and kissed that frozen body on the cheek, and realized then that the Dad I knew was definitely not inside that corpse. For years afterwards, I always remembered having to kiss that dead body. Sometimes I dreamt about it. I would never kiss anyone in a coffin again.

CHAPTER SEVEN

Moving On

> *"We were very sad about having to leave our new Indian grandmother and uncles."*

It was not long after that, maybe a few weeks, when Michael and I were told that we were going away and would soon get a new mom and dad. Mom didn't want to take care of us any more, now that Dad had died. My uncles and grandmother all said good-bye to us before we left. We were very sad about having to leave our new Indian grandmother and uncles, but with Dad now dead, we didn't really mind not having to live with that mom.

After saying goodbye to our grandmother and uncles, Michael, Mom and I took a trip to a little town nearby. After we walked into an office building, Mom went to talk with some people in another room, and Michael and I were told to sit in the waiting room. While we waited, we started playing a guessing game, because we thought we were soon going to meet our new mom and dad. Through the glass doors and windows we could see men and women coming up the sidewalk outside. Some would come into the waiting room and we thought, *"Oh my; this must be them!"* We whispered to each other, thinking that maybe they were just coming to check us out to see what we were like. Michael and I then came up with a plan; we decided if we liked the man and woman we saw, we would act really nice. If we thought they were mean-looking people, we would act like we were bad boys. A number of couples came and went while we waited. We were sad when we realized the nice ones were there for another reason, and we were very happy when the mean-looking ones left without us. Quite some time later, Mom came out of the room she had been in and said good-bye to both Michael and me. I saw her crying as she went out the door. That was sort of sad.

As it turned out, Mom had dropped us off at Social Services in Geraldton, Ontario. From there we were transported to the twin cities of Port Arthur and Fort William (today called Thunder Bay). We were placed in a very large facility with many children, known as the Children's Aid Society. Michael and I sort of liked that place—not as many rules and lots of kids to play with.

"We only acted nice if we wanted to get picked."

Every few days or so, the children were put in a long line-up, and new moms and dads would walk up and down the line, talking to all the kids and trying to decide which one they wanted. Michael and I always stood really close together; when they talked to us, we always told them right away that we were brothers, because we didn't want to get split up. We also played the game we had learned in that waiting room that day. We only acted nice if we wanted to get picked, and we pushed and shoved each other and acted bad when we didn't like the looks of the man and woman.

One day, we all went skating on a big lake. Wow, what a skating rink! (I later found out it was Lake Superior.) We went there quite a bit; and that's where Michael and I both learned how to skate. The school wasn't too bad there; but I had to walk to it. I remember two things very clearly about that school: I got the strap on my hands twice, once in front of the whole class for talking in class, and the other time it was in the principal's office. Because I got the strap, I became quite popular with the kids in the class; they asked me how much the strap hurt and if I wanted to cry.

One boy told me that the next time I was going to be strapped I should put a hair on my hand. Then when the strap hit my hand it would cause the hair to cut me and cause my hand to bleed. The teacher would then have to stop, and would probably feel bad about hitting so hard. I thought that was a pretty good plan.

Well, the next time soon came. I was a little late for school one day, and as I came near the school building I had to pee very badly. I knew I couldn't make it into the school without peeing my pants. No one was outside the school when I arrived, because the bell had rung; so I peed up against the back of the school. When I finished, I saw one of the teachers looking around the corner of the school watching me. This time I was marched into a separate room with the principal, and as I was being led to the office I was trying to pull a hair off my head. Just before she started swinging the strap, I put the hair on my hand and hoped for the best; but it didn't bleed and I wasn't sure what happened to the hair. That strap really hurt a lot that time, and if I hadn't just peed up against the back of the school, I probably would have peed my pants because of the licking I got. I decided I didn't want any more straps.

One day the adults running the Children's Aid centre asked Michael and me if we still remembered our Uncle Andy and Aunt Helene from our days on the farm. I said I remembered uncle Andy really well, because he had always brought us candy when he visited us on the farm. They told us that Uncle Andy and Aunt Helene wanted us to go and live with them. Wow! We were super excited. Michael and I talked in bed until late that night, trying to remember things about them. We couldn't wait to go. A few days later, we were on a train traveling with a lady who took care of us on the trip. I remember us finally arriving at the train station; and boy, were we ever excited! When we got off the train, I ran down the platform as fast as I could, looking all over for Uncle Andy; and I was a bit disappointed in myself when I realized I had run right past him. He called Michael and me back, and gave us a big hug. In his pocket he had some candy for us. Wow, just like old times! This was just great!

We drove to Stratton that night, and walked into what was to be our new home. Well, Michael and I were absolutely in seventh heaven when we saw that two of our sisters, Sophie and Patsy, were standing there waiting for us—they lived there too; wow! This was just the greatest thing ever. We were going to be living with two of our sisters. This was going to be just great!

I was now nine years old, and nine years away from my first attack....

CHAPTER EIGHT

That Little Bag

Gord MacNeil on the left
Author on the right

Gord and I had met at boot camp in Cornwallis, Nova Scotia in 1970, and became the best of friends; it would be a friendship that would last the rest of our lives. On completion of basic training, we were both posted to the same naval ships in Esquimalt, British Columbia; and us both having picked the same naval trade (Sonarman), we most often were on the same training courses. In January of 1973, both Gord and I, with a few other great navy buddies—Rodney (he was called Red); our French buddy, Bernie; Jay, Lou, and other mates—were all posted to HMCS Restigouche. The Restigouche, however, was still in Halifax; therefore our west coast ship's company had to fly to Halifax to sail the ship via the Panama Canal, to bring her around to join the west coast fleet. It took longer than expected to get the ship to a state of operational readiness prior to sailing; so we ended up spending six months in Halifax. As fate would have it, Gord, Red and I all met our wives-to-be; so after the ship finally arrived in Esquimalt, BC, the three of us returned to Halifax within a couple of months to marry our brides and bring them back west.

In the fall of 1977, our naval careers would see to it that most of us buddies would finally part ways. I was posted back to the east coast to serve on *HMCS Huron*.

Prior to heading back east, Ellen and I decided to visit some of my family in the Vancouver area, and also drop in to see Gord at his brother's apartment. We were looking to reminisce about old times and say our goodbyes, prior to parting ways. We were having some good chuckles at the kitchen table when Gord came back from the bathroom, tapped me on the shoulder and asked me to follow him. At the door of the bedroom he told me, "Look inside." Lo and behold, there stood Gord's mom. I was perplexed: why did he have his mom hidden in the bedroom? She nicely asked me to come in and sit down, so I did. She asked me, "So tell me, Jim, about this demon that spoke to you." Gord smiled, closed the door and left his mom and me alone. It had been well over a year since Gord had made that promise I had requested of

HMCS Restigouche

him—to arrange a meeting with his mom, that I would have to attend—and he had kept that promise.

After describing to Gord's mom some of the torments I was experiencing, and what that *thing* sounded like, she actually told me its name. Today, I've forgotten what that name was; but back then, I thought, "Wow! She knew that ugly thing's *name*?" She was able to name a few other demons that she felt might be deceiving me, as well. I thought again: "Wow! Not only does she believe what I'm telling her, but those things actually have names! And I'm not crazy after all!" I knew I had picked the right person. The more Gord's mom spoke to me, the more optimistic I became, that she may also have a solution to help me control these torments; and I couldn't wait to hear what that was.

Before we parted, she said she would pray for me, and suggested that I pray also. I thought to myself, *"Hmm? Pray? Pray what?"* I was taught to memorize a few prayers as a child; but that was about it. She then pulled a tiny little book out of her purse and handed it to me. She said I should read it when I could; but most important, she said, was to always keep the little book on me—to keep it in my pocket, and also to go to bed with it at night, if need be. The book was a miniature Gideon's Bible, she said it was the "Word" of God—and the demons hated and feared it.

As months and years passed, I don't remember ever reading that little book; but it did become like a best friend to me, because keeping it on my person definitely worked. I even found a little cloth bag for it, with a string to keep the top closed; that way, I could keep it hidden from others. After all, it wasn't very manly, especially for a seasoned sailor, to be going around with a Bible in his pocket. And what would I ever say to someone, if they asked why I was carrying it around? *"I'm fending off demons?"* Hmmm, I don't think so. So I kept it well hidden; and what was in that little bag was my little secret.

When I did find myself again under attack, from time to time, I would realize that my little bag was not with me. Damn it, I had forgotten to take it again! Or I left it in my other coat pocket. When going on a trip, that little book became much more important to me than remembering to take my toothbrush. That little bag travelled halfway around the world and back with me.

The little bag the demons hated

Whenever I felt the conditions might have unfolded for an attack to be imminent, I would go out of my way to ensure that the little bag was close by my side. In fact, at times I remember getting into my truck and going back to get it.

*"I was…comforted in knowing **it** couldn't touch me tonight."*

Bedtime or naptime, I knew, were the most crucial times; just prior to dozing off to sleep had to be my weakest moment, when I became most vulnerable to those horrific attacks. The evil presence seemed to know exactly the moment to slither in for the capture; there appeared to be only a small window of opportunity when it was able to strike—and far too often, it was successful. I came to realize that, for whatever reason, it didn't try to *envelop* (capture) me when I was fully conscious and in control. Also, I realized that if I were successful in falling asleep normally, I would have a normal night's rest. However, it was those critical fifteen seconds or so—between being awake and falling into a peaceful sleep— that were so haunting; it was in that short window of opportunity that it always made its move. I would often lie in bed at night con- templating the arrival of those critical seconds, and wondering if

I'd make it through to a normal night's rest—or would I be engaged in another battle. Lying in bed, I'd often hold the little bag tight on my chest under my tee shirt, right next to my skin, and be comforted in knowing *it* couldn't touch me tonight.

PERPLEXED

"Blackouts were the very thing...I'd never drink to the extent of having."

Years rolled by, and my naval postings changed back and forth from various ships to land units. I worked hard, and I was promoted up the ladder quite rapidly. I also played hard—often too hard. I suffered the consequences of playing hard, with hangovers and the more painful experience of being told of the stupid things I had done the night before. Blackouts. Yes, I recall that when I was a teenager, blackouts were the very thing I once told my oldest brother I'd never drink to the extent of having.

Weekend partying at our home in Antrim, Nova Scotia happened far too often; the second and even third day after a Saturday night drinking party would always find me physically exhausted, as well as emotionally and mentally fatigued—the perfect conditions for an attack. A few sailor friends, to whom I had entrusted (in part) what my torments were about, told me that the attacks I had were probably the DT's (Delirium Tremens), which is an acute episode of delirium usually caused by withdrawal from alcohol. I responded to them that my attacks had started long before I started to abuse or even to drink alcohol; and it was the attacks that would at times compel me to drink myself to sleep. This, obviously, was a "solution" that always backfired. In effect, alcohol only postponed the misery for that one evening—and then increased the likelihood and frequency of the attacks for two or three days afterwards. I later became convinced that the attacks were a good reason *not* to have hang-overs, because it was simply inviting more frequent trouble.

A NEW ATTACKER

"This new development was incredibly disappointing."

A few years later, a new type of attack started. Sometimes after work, driving home to Antrim in my orange Datsun, I would have "company" in my truck: a voice would start talking up a storm. It seemed that about fifteen minutes into my trip home, when I was getting close to Miller Lake, it would start its annoying arguments. There was no one physically in the truck with me; but there was certainly an uninvited and definite voice. My first thought about this voice was that it might be my own mind thinking out loud. Really loud, at that. The voice, which was obviously resident in my head, was very real and clear, speaking more audibly than if someone were sitting in the passenger seat, talking to me. The voice always had one ultimate sugges-tion: it would tell me that all the problems I was struggling over would be solved if I simply went home and killed my wife. I was stunned. I would argue back that Ellen had done nothing wrong, and the problems I was dealing with and the suffering I was going through were of my own creation and nothing to do with Ellen. At first I was shocked that I had allowed my thoughts to wander off to such ridiculousness. Where in hell did that voice come from? The reasoning didn't even make sense. Then I thought, *"My God, was this some kind of residue in my brain as a result of my childhood experiences? Is this the same voice that had tormented my Dad?"*

This new development was incredibly disappointing. I could see that things in my life were getting worse, not better; and I couldn't believe this was happening. Why in hell did this new torment have to start? And how much of this nonsense, coupled with all those other sporadic torments, could my mind take and still remain sane? How much can any mind take before it cracks? I was haunted by thinking that this may have been the kind of compounded torment that drove my Dad to his fatal end, after first taking the life of my mother. Surely it had to be similar. The urgency to ensure that it wouldn't break me had increased significantly; I had to find a solution—fast.

Again and again, the voice would remind me of all my past, incredibly justifying some of the terrible and foolish things I had done—things my wife didn't know about, and things she would be furious about if she ever found out. The voice would tell me that I had worked hard and deserved to do those things, and I didn't deserve these problems and this torment. It would tell me that I was a good person, and that I only had to kill my wife, and all my problems would be solved. Because it was only my wife who would be upset; so if I removed her, I wouldn't have to fear being found out.

Over the next few weeks, I started again to analyze this new phenomenon, and concluded that this *voice* was not of my doing at all; it just wanted me to *think* it was. It was, in fact, something else that was resident in my head—something that I didn't seem to have any control over, to make it shut up. At least not yet.

"I wanted so much just to have a normal life." Encouragingly, it seemed that once I had concluded that the voice in my head didn't belong to me, that *the voice* also realized that I had figured it out. It then carelessly and openly exposed itself as its own separate being. That is to say, its deception was exposed, so it came out of hiding; it abandoned the deception of *trying to make me think it was my own mind*, and

instead now it just attacked openly—and with a vengeance! It became much more belligerent and forceful, and would start screaming at me in the truck on the way home. I saw that it had become very angry. *"Get out of my life and get out of my head!"* I would scream back.

My God, I wanted so much to just have a normal life! Surely other people don't suffer from these types of torments, and have to be hiding them, as I was! It was a lonely place to be in, not being able to tell someone else. Who could be trusted to know this?

I realized that I needed a solution, and I needed it *now!* Alcohol, I knew, increased the frequency of the other tormentor; so I couldn't revert to that. I didn't believe in drugs or dope, and I certainly couldn't trust a soul about the nature of this new development; so I was trapped. It was up to me to find the solution or else.

"My asking God for help had always preceded insightful solutions that popped into my head."

It is often quoted that *"There are no atheists in foxholes"*—especially if you are being shot at during a war. During those times, atheists have been known to turn to God for help. I was now in that same type of desperate situation, and forced to humble myself; I called out to God.

Having been forced to rely on God as the only reliable resource for lesser situations in the past—and then breaking my promises to Him so many times—had made me ashamed to approach Him yet again. But I had nowhere else to turn.

"If you are real, and wherever you are, God, please, please help me; because this thing, this voice in my head is nothing less then demonic!"

I realized some years later that my asking God for help had always preceded insightful solutions that popped into my head.

It was the next day, on my way home from work, that I thought of an idea: when I neared Miller Lake, I was ready this time to confront the voice; and sure enough, it showed up on schedule. It was almost like picking up a hitchhiker.

When it started its repeated rhetoric, I immediately spoke to it aloud: I said, "*I know who you are and you will immediately stop accusing my wife and stop talking to me. From now on, I promise you that every time you open your mouth I will say the Lord's Prayer out loud in the truck. So, devil, you decide how many times you want me to pray today, and every day.*"

I wasn't a religious person, but in the days when I was in school, we said the Lord's Prayer every day, so I remembered the words. This obviously infuriated the voice and it started screaming at me. I immediately started screaming the Lord's Prayer out loud in the truck: "*Our Father which art in heaven, Hallowed be thy name. Thy kingdom come....*" I screamed the whole prayer, loud enough that I couldn't hear the voice trying to scream back. Once I completed the prayer, the voice kicked in again; so again I recited the Lord's Prayer; and again, and again, and again. The voice was obviously testing to see if I would tire, but I didn't give up. On the first day, I was almost home before this first battle ended. The voice, for whatever reason, never bothered me other than when I was driving home. On the days that followed, the same routine would happen; but each day, it shut up a little sooner.

I had friends and family say to me that they had passed me on the highway, they had waved to me, honked their horn, but I appeared to be singing out loud in my truck and never did notice them. Yes, at times I do sing aloud in my truck; but on some of those occasions I knew I was in the middle of a battle and hollering out the Lord's Prayer. I simply admitted to friends and family that I'd been preoccupied by singing.

"Well, devil, it's time to pray isn't it?"

After a couple weeks, as I neared Miller Lake on my way home, I got to the point where I would even taunt the voice before it started to speak to me: *"Well, devil, it's time to pray isn't it? How many times do you want me to pray today?"* I would encourage it to expose itself. Sure enough, it would speak up and try some other lying approach to get me interested in what it had to say—and I immediately started to pray, *"Our Father who art in heaven..."*—I would laugh at it and tell it how much I loved to pray... *"Please talk to me so I can start praying,"* I'd plead. After a few weeks, the voice would no longer respond to my taunts. It didn't return, and my memories of it faded.

POSTINGS

At the rank of Chief Petty Officer, Second Class, in about the year 1986, I was posted to Saint John, New Brunswick as part of the Naval Quality Assurance contingent to oversee the building of our new City Class destroyers at the Saint John Shipyards. My responsibility was mainly in the installation and grooming of the Combat Systems equipment on each new ship. This turned out to be a four-year posting, after which my wife, son, daughter and I returned to Nova Scotia and bought a home in Lantz. Just prior to returning to Nova Scotia, my wife and I made the decision to change our name back to my birth name. Because of the questions our children were asking, we found in so doing, it was easier for us to explain to them our family roots.

I was posted to the Naval Engineering Unit Atlantic (NEU) in Dartmouth, and shortly after my arrival, the 1990 Gulf War became imminent. The preparations took me for a short but "high alert" deployment to Dubai in the United Arab Emirates, to help with electronic modification that needed to be completed on our ships that had already arrived in the Gulf. It was the day before the first tomahawk missile was fired at Baghdad, and our mission being just completed, it was decided that our team was to be flown home. Once home, it took at least three to four days' rest before my adrenaline levels returned to what I would consider normal. I found it interesting how one's body goes into high alert without actually realizing how much, until after one is back home and out of immediate danger. I was physically and emotionally drained because of operating in a war-type arena for a couple of weeks. Once I was safe and resting at home, I was also mentally exhausted—and therefore again a prime candidate for that other tormentor to pick up its frequency of attacks. The *tingling* would start, and again the ongoing battle over the destruction of my mind would ensue.

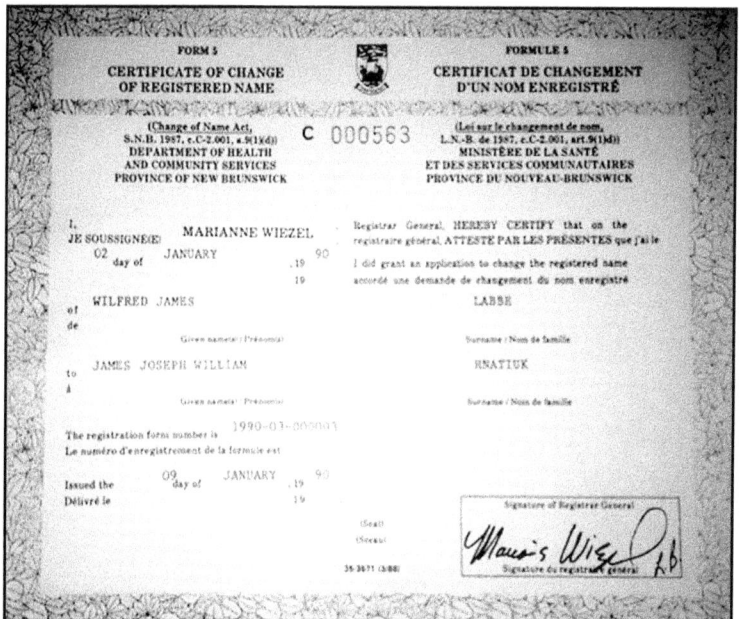

Certificate of Name Change, January 2nd, 1990

CHAPTER NINE

Prelude to Transition

"My expertise was in combat systems."

My stay with N.E.U. Atlantic was short-lived, and I was soon posted to "Sea Training Staff, Atlantic" within Maritime Command. This small but very prestigious team was the envy of many in the fleet, as we were responsible to test every ship's company's ability to achieve combat readiness, prior to them being released for operational deployments. Each Sea Trainer had a specific area of responsibility, and my expertise was in combat systems electronics, such as would be found in sonars, radars, missile systems, electronic warfare, etc. This assignment took me on numerous trips to sea during the various stages of testing.

Because of my consistently high yearly performance evaluations, my immediate supervisor and the unit Commanding Officer both highly recommended to Headquarters in Ottawa that I be considered for Commissioning from the

Author CPO1 Jim Hnatiuk awarded the NATO Special Service Medal

Ranks (CFR). If successful, I would be promoted to the rank of Lieutenant. Ottawa agreed with these recommendations, and in turn offered me the opportunity to sit the CFR Board tests; I decided to sit the Board; I passed, and made the grade to be commissioned. That year, however, the quota for CFR officers in Combat Systems Engineering was low, so I was asked to wait until the following year to be commissioned.

During that waiting period, I was promoted to the prestigious rank of Chief Petty Officer, First Class (CPO1), which is the most senior non-commissioned rank in the Royal Canadian Navy. As a result, when the year was up, I decided to not re-apply for my commission and instead to live out the rest of my career as a CPO1.

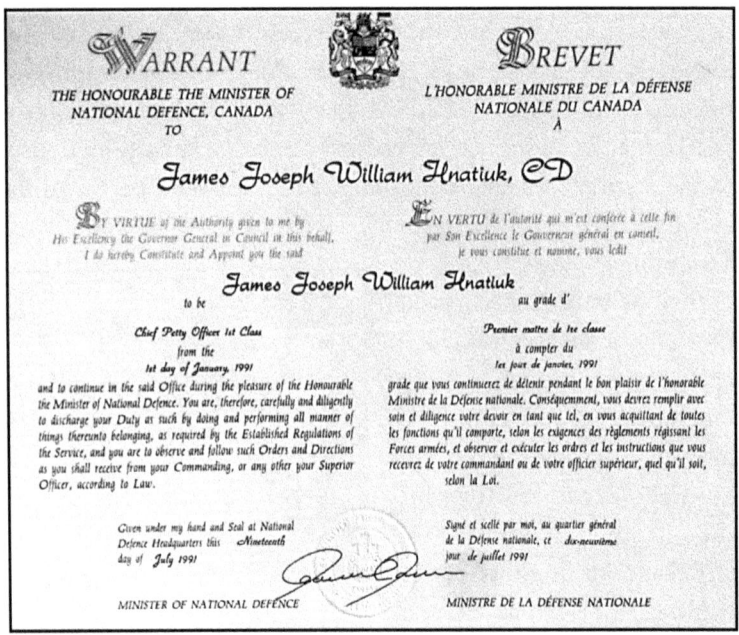

The Author's recognized promotion to the highest non-commissioned rank in the Canadian Armed Forces, signed by the Minister of National Defense.

> *"The tormentor didn't care what my rank got to be."*

It's important to understand that regardless of the on-again, off-again visits of the tormentor, it didn't prevent me from performing at a very high level, and achieving significant job promotions as a result. One thing was for certain, though: the tormentor didn't care what my rank got to be, and I'd often be found looking for that "little bag" to keep on my person. There was many times, however, that I'd be caught without the book—and suffered the consequences.

On one such occasion, I recall being trapped inside my lifeless corpse and forced to watch as dark demon-like persons moved around in my bedroom and around the bed I was lying on. These hooded, dark figures groaned, taunted and tormented me, and appeared to be anticipating my demise. For reasons I can't explain, I felt that some time soon they'd have permission to do whatever they wanted with me. This was certainly concerning, and caused me, sometimes, to believe that I might be losing this lifelong battle.

My little bag with the Gideon's Bible appeared to have suddenly lost its power for fending off the tormentors; and not understanding why, nor investigating it further, I had to resort to another plan. It's important that you understand that at this point in my life, I was not a religious person; in my ignorance, I probably would have claimed to the right audience that I was religious; but I had zero prayer life or church participation, and my only pursuit of God was when I was confronted by these horrific and sudden attacks. So with the little book not performing as it had any more, my Plan B was to start using what I knew had worked for me in the past, and that was to call on God.

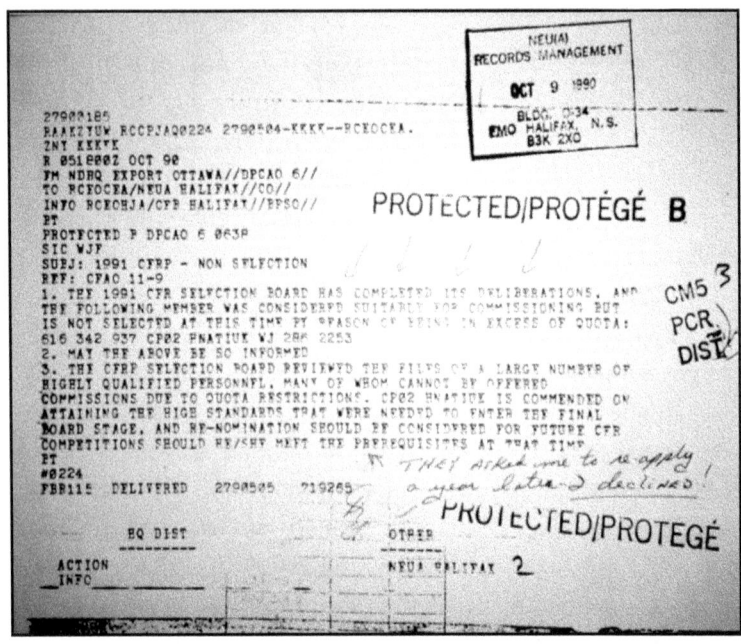

Message from National Defence Headquarters, October 9th, 1990, stating that the author is commended on attaining the high standard required for commissioning but quota restrictions prevented it from going ahead that year.

> *"When I say try to scream, I mean scream with every ounce of energy my spirit could muster up!"*

The Lord's Prayer had worked for fending off the *voice* tormentor, so I figured that using God again in some capacity seemed to make sense for the other tormentor(s). So now, during each attack, when I was trapped inside my corpse right after being suddenly terrorized, I would labour to start screaming out the name of Jesus. When I say try to scream, I mean scream with every ounce of energy my spirit could muster up! My escape from each entrapment continued to be a great struggle, and took much mental and physical effort, as now, the shock factor of each attack was growing in intensity. The same name that I had so often used to curse at someone, I was now instead asking Him to help me; I didn't care to figure out why screaming the name of Jesus helped—I was going to use whatever worked. The name appeared to have a companion effect in the darkness, and certainly seemed to work to lessen the grip of the attacker.

It was at sea, on board one of the destroyers during *a* sea training workups that I decided to relax in the Chiefs' and Petty Officers' lounge prior to retiring for the night. I sat down beside my friend Kenny, who was engulfed in a book he was reading. Kenny was a fellow Chief Petty Officer; he was also someone I had come to respect, and someone I knew I could truly confide in whenever the need arose. The book he was reading that evening was of con-

siderable size; intrigued, I asked what he was reading. "It's called *Evidence that Demands a Verdict*, by Josh McDowell," he said.

"The book had been written for university students."

I asked him what it was about. He explained it was a book that hypothetically put Jesus Christ on trial in a modern-day courtroom. He explained that all the historical evidence about Christ was presented and argued, as it would be for any other case in today's courts; and in the end, the jury would have to decide whether Jesus' claims to be the Son of

God were true. He explained that the book had been written for university students, and it had a very complete set of the historical references in the second half of the book.

In my ignorance, because of what I was taught as a child, I challenged him with the question: "So, Kenny, you don't really believe there's a God, do you? You have to read books to try convince yourself that there is a God?" To which Kenny replied, "Jim, the Bible says to love the Lord your God with all of your heart, all of your soul, all of your mind, and all of your strength. How can you love God with all of your mind, if you don't read and study to satisfy your mind?"

I thought for a moment and then said, "Hmm...is *that* what that means?"

"It was absolutely the last thing the devil in me wanted me to find out about!"

On the surface, what Kenny said to me may appear to most to be pretty insignificant; but I can assure you, it was anything but that to me. I later realized that it was absolutely the last thing the devil in me wanted me to find out about! But now that I knew, the big secret was out: all the lies I had been taught to believe as truth since childhood had been exposed. I couldn't have imagined how Kenny's simple explanation would now change the entire course of everything in my life.

"You mean I'm allowed to question and study those things I don't understand about God?" The thought of what he had said wouldn't leave me.

So what am I talking about? You see, during my "Christian" upbringing as a child, I was taught not to ask too many questions about God; that asking questions was a sign of doubt, and something only weak Christians do. As a child, I was made to believe that there were a lot of mysteries about God, and it wasn't my place to question them. This was so well embedded in my mind that I actually thought it was a sin to question what I was taught about my faith. So my entire concept of God up to that point in my life was built on *blind* faith; and now, as a young adult, I would argue, with arrogance and in ignorance, that my belief in God was strong. I felt that because others wanted to study the Bible, that that was a sign of weakness; and what they were trying to figure out was really a mystery anyway, so why waste your time? Simply believe like I did—right?

Another attraction of my blind faith was that my slowly eroding concept of God didn't come with very many absolutes. I found myself being able to rationalize the foundation in religion that I had been given as a boy, and simply change the rules to suit my fancy. Given time, I found ways to compromise between what was good and what was bad. After a while, some of the things that originally were bad weren't so bad after all; and then, after I'd indulged in them enough times, it began to seem (to me) that some really weren't bad *at all*.

When I found myself crossing the border into what I still considered sin, I would simply promise God (just in case He really existed) that I wouldn't do it again if He'd let me get away with it *just this one last time*. I'd passionately and honestly ask Him to give me a break, and I was even embarrassed when I'd confront Him again six months or a year later, promising the same old thing all over again.

> "My biggest concern in this ill-conceived plan was that I would have to see death coming to pull it off."

And so, in my ill-fated understanding of life, I really believed that if I were about to die, I'd simply have to ask quickly for forgiveness for anything I had done wrong; and if heaven really existed, then off I'd go to enjoy eternity! And if heaven didn't exist, nothing was lost. My biggest concern in this ill-conceived plan was that I would have to see death coming to pull it off, because I'd need at least thirty seconds or so to recite the "act of contrition" that I was taught as a boy, so that all my sins would be forgiven. If I failed in that endeavour, I could see myself being permanently subjected to the very same hell I had periodically been experiencing in that "other dimension" for nearly thirty years.

God forbid! I couldn't imagine living eternally under such torment!

TWO IMPORTANT FACTORS

It's only in being allowed the luxury of looking back that I'm able to understand the transition that had started to take place. Two very important factors now came into play: First, the discovery of knowing that I could (without sinning) investigate the core of my faith; and second, the tormentor's change of tactics as a result of my new pursuit. (I'll describe the second point in detail later.)

> "My quest for knowledge about everything I didn't understand... now became my targets, and my absolute focus."

My quest for knowledge about everything I didn't understand, and about obstacles that stood in the way of making God and the Bible fully believable, now became my targets, and my absolute focus. Evolution, the speed of light, Adam and Eve, Noah's flood, scientific evidences, hypocrisy in churches and in so-called "born-again" Christians—you name it, I couldn't seem to get my hands on enough books to satisfy my new thirst. It was refreshing, knowing that none of this investigation was disallowed; and that, in fact, God *wanted* my mind to be satisfied. Over the next six months to a year, my entire belief system was undergoing a major transition, as I dove from one book to the next. As soon as my mind was satisfied on one subject, I'd immediately be driven to another.

One subject that captured my attention—and bothered me so much that I continued to study it for about eight years after my initial investigations—was evolution. After just a few months, and extensive research on the theory of evolution, I could hardly believe what I was discovering!

> *"I was actually wondering whether I could sue the Ontario school board for allowing me to be taught such lies!"*

I soon became quite angry about having been taught evolution as being a fact in grade school, because I now discovered that it's no more than a myth—an unproven theory. I was actually wondering whether I could sue the Ontario school board for allowing me to be taught such lies! I was angry, because I now realized how effective such teachings had been in allowing my faith to be challenged and weakened over my entire life…and to find out now that the complete reverse is true!

It's incredible that thousands of scientists will attest to their belief in Intelligent Design, and that they have written untold books on the facts that support their conclusions, *yet there is never a mention of that in any public school books.* Why was it that both Evolution and Intelligent Design cannot be taught to children? Then let *them* decide which they wish to believe. Later, in my years of research on the subject, I watched a video interview in which an evolutionary scientist was asked a very similar question. The interviewer asked, "If both Evolution and Intelligent Design were taught in a classroom, which do you think would have the stronger arguments?" Incredibly, he—an atheist—answered, "Intelligent Design would win, hands down." That admission, coming from a scientist who worked in the field of evolution—and also being an atheist—speaks volumes.

The more I studied, the more my eyes were opened to how an atheistic minority in our society has infiltrated and permeated our educational, judicial and parliamentary systems. Not because their arguments were based on better facts, but rather because they don't believe in God, so they push their own agenda and unsupported theories! People of faith didn't fight back to the degree necessary, so we now have what we deserve.

> *"Let me encourage you: this gets a lot **better**."*

I could see now how the impact of evolutionary brainwashing, especially on impressionable children, quickly grows and entraps an unsuspecting society into oblivion. If the few untruths I was told as a child negatively impacted my belief system to the extent that it did, consider the two generations after me, and how they have been intentionally disillusioned by our school system! If you're one of those from the generations after mine, and you're reading this book, you may very well be having difficulty believing the last three or four paragraphs I've written. Let me encourage you: this gets a lot *better*; so read on and risk being exposed to the truth; because you couldn't be any more surprised about all this than I was.

What do I mean by saying "This gets a lot better"? Read on!

CHAPTER TEN

Preamble to Miracles

Before I drag your convictions through some of the very important steps that completed my metamorphosis, and describe what I did that finally defeated the tormentor, I'll first jump ahead a number years to some of my miracle years—and return later to share with you what I consider were my final transitional years, and the secrets that made the transition possible.

> "The demonic is very effective in its deceptive ability in presenting itself as being 'divine.'"

You should know, as well, that having been fooled, deceived and tormented by the demonic for approximately thirty years, my ability to determine the difference between what is demonic and what is divine is very good. I'm not being unfair when I say that most people would find this task very difficult; and I mention this because the demonic is very effective in its deceptive ability in presenting itself as being "divine" and/or an "angel of light."

Please understand that the demonic consistently presents itself, or the situation it creates for you, as beautiful, intriguing, the smart thing to do; at times seductive and *always* inviting. Then, as long as you're being deceived—as long as you're unsuspecting— there's little or no reason for it to show its true, horrific nature. But then, of course, if it sees you becoming a potential threat to his work, he may decide to "take you out" by giving you a taste of what he gave me for nearly thirty years. Bottom line: don't think for a minute that you're the exception to the rule, and won't be (or currently are not) one of its targets; that's total illusion.

With the beautiful, intriguing, and inviting situations it creates, it will slowly and carefully twist and corrupt each one over time, to eventually ensure that you and/or someone you love or loved will be its next victim. Satan isn't called "the master of deception" and "the father of lies" for no reason; and his patience to do this will certainly outlast ours.

My knowledge and ability today to discern what's evil within the supernatural, and what's good, comes as a result of experiencing both in a major capacity. You'll see this, as I am now about to share what truly were astonishing and miraculous encounters with God and with angels.

Know this: both what's good and what's evil at the onset can look and feel quite similar; but in time, the difference between the two becomes undeniable. Am I saying that the demonic can look and feel like something miraculous? Yes, absolutely; and it's almost always presented as such. It's only because I was repeatedly fooled and enveloped, first within the demonic for many years, and then later the miraculous—and both over long periods of time—that allows me the confidence to make any such claim now.

No one could ever convince me that my miraculous encounters were demonic; and after I share with you some of those encounters in the next few chapters, I hope you'll be totally convinced of this, as well. It's because I have come to not only recognize the enemy's abilities, but also to have lived through them for so many years, that I can make these claims. The need for much scrutiny and discernment cannot be over-emphasized. Is it possible that I can still be deceived? Absolutely! I'll never take anything for granted. But I'll be sharing with you ways that can reduce or even prevent the possibility of that happening.

> "You may really be starting to wonder who this author is."

You may really be starting to wonder who this author is, claiming he knows such things. Can I be trusted as a reliable source? Or am I some kind of a madman, ready for the insane asylum? In response, I have to trust that the members of my family, my friends, employees, and colleagues, who know me well, will testify to the fact that I am a credible and a very reliable source. Secondly, not to boast, but please allow some of my accomplishments in life thus far to add a bit to my credibility:

- I was promoted to the highest non-commissioned rank in the Canadian military, and even achieved the grades to become a commissioned officer.

- In just the last decade, I was elected leader of the Christian Heritage Party of Canada (the sixth largest federal party in Canada) and served in that capacity from 2008 to 2014. *www.chp.ca*

- As an entrepreneur (with zero start-up funding), in nine years I built, from the ground up, a business currently worth well over two million dollars, of which I am currently President and Co-owner. *www.hnatiuks.com*

- I am the Training Director of Hnatiuk's Training Division Ltd. in Lantz, NS, Canada, which currently is the provider of all Hunter Education and Firearms courses for the province of Nova Scotia. *www.hnatiukstraining.com*

- I am currently the Chair of the Board of Directors at Emmanuel Baptist Church in Upper Hammonds Plains, NS. My Overseer is the Rev. Dr. Lennett J. Anderson. *www.ebcmeet.com*

- I'm a husband, happily married to Ellen for forty-two years, father and grandfather, and truly blessed today by the harmony and beauty within our family.

I'm not speaking from the perspective of someone who is disillusioned or searching for answers, nor someone who is trying to figure out inexplicable phenomena. Nor am I looking for accolades, sympathy or praise; my purpose for writing is much greater than any of those goals.

"You can rest assured that what I've experienced and what I'm sharing with you is accurate."

After close to forty-eight years of dealing with the good and evil powers within the supernatural, you can rest assured that what I've experienced and what I'm sharing with you is accurate, and that I write with much care. I do this with a sound mind, and for a very good and important purpose. You can be confident that I am no one's fool; but rather that I know precisely what I have encountered and what I continue to encounter. As you can well imagine, I'm taking certain risks in sharing these things with you, given the positions I've attained and have held or currently hold; but I believe that at my age, the benefits this project offers outweigh those risks. I unashamedly and wholeheartedly share it with you now, so that anyone who wishes can most certainly benefit. To what extent you benefit will be entirely up to you. If you use the information I provide in this book, I'm convinced that some day you'll really be thankful that you did. If you dismiss it, that's your choice; but I believe it will be one you'll regret.

CHAPTER ELEVEN

The "4:44" Miracle

As I mentioned, I'll return a little later to share with you the *key* that allowed me to move from torment to miracles; but first, it's important that I jump ahead a number years to describe some of the miracles that accompanied that major transition.

> *"I figured I could catapult myself years ahead simply by reading books."*

This particular miracle happened only a couple of years after I had initiated my search for knowledge on every question about God. My quest, at this point, was still ongoing; but now, to get a jump on things, I sought out books about what other influential people had encountered about God in their life journeys. After all, I figured, why try and find something out for yourself if numerous people before you already lived it and were willing to share it with you in books? I was now in my late forties; and to make up for lost time, I figured I could catapult myself years ahead simply by reading books from authors such as Billy Graham, Tommy Tenney, Neil Armstrong, Grant Jeffrey and a dozen others of that calibre. In every case, what intrigued me most was their testimony of the Godly encounters they'd had and/or the "miracles" they said had happened in their lives. It was that type of evidence and testimonies that I needed in my life now, to quench my thirst for knowledge. So my question was: what did they do that I wasn't doing, to get those close encounters with God?

I don't recall the particular author, but I do recall snippets of a story that was shared in one of those books that piqued my interest, and eventually opened the door to my "4:44 miracle." The author gave an account of witnessing to a prisoner who was an atheist, and very skeptical of the whole concept of God. After numerous failed attempts, the author decided to give it one last try before abandoning all hope of helping this prisoner. Before departing from what he felt would be his last visit with the inmate, he challenged the prisoner to prove to himself that God is real. When the prisoner asked how he could possibly do that, the author told him: "Ask God to do something for you. Ask God to wake you up at a certain time in the night, and see whether or not He will." The story then described how the prisoner did exactly what the author had suggested, and ended up having a God encounter that he could never have imagined—one that was life-transforming for that prisoner.

> *"So having nothing to lose…I decided to give it a try."*

Very intrigued by this story, I thought to myself: "Why not me?" If God would do that for some bad guy doing time in prison, surely He'd do it for me, too…right? It wasn't like I hadn't spent a little time behind bars as a young misbehaving sailor, to straighten me out. I had, so I could relate to this story in more ways than one.

So having nothing to lose, and really without too much hope or expectation of anything significant happening, I decided to give it a try. *Tonight,* I thought, *I'm going to ask God to wake me up in the middle of the night.* I just had to figure out what time I'd ask Him to do that. The time I chose, I knew, would be very important; because if this worked, I didn't want to think later that it was some kind of fluke or coincidence, and thus bring doubt into the whole thing and spoil it!

The time I decided on was forty-four minutes after the hour. So, in some quiet time alone in my bedroom before going to bed that night, I simply asked God, "If You're real, I really want to know it; and I need to see something tangible. So I'm asking You, God, to show me by waking me up in the middle of the night. Wake me up at forty-four minutes after the hour. I don't care what hour, but only that my digital clock will show me that it's forty-four minutes after the hour when You wake me up."

So with that simple prayer I soon dozed off to sleep. As it turned out, I didn't wake up during that night, but instead woke up in the morning as normal. I felt a little foolish about the request I had made; I got up and went to work.

As it happened, on the second night, I was sound asleep, in the wee small hours of the morning, when my eyes suddenly opened. I noticed that my wife was still sound asleep, so whatever had awakened me hadn't disturbed her. Having no clue why I woke up, I simply rolled over to go back to sleep. When I rolled over, I was facing my digital clock, and my eye caught a glimpse of the time. It was 4:44 a.m.

I opened one eye again, just for a couple of seconds, to be sure of what I'd seen, and then closed it again. It was indeed 4:44 a.m. As I dozed off to sleep again, I was briefly reminded of what I had asked for, and I thought, "Hmmm…what are the odds of that happening just by chance?" When I woke up in the morning, I briefly recalled what had happened during the night, and I brushed it off as a coincidence…until a few days later….

"It was sort of like losing a bet, and not really knowing what you owed the other person."

Again, nothing appeared to be out of the ordinary. I was sound asleep in bed, when suddenly my eyes opened wide; something had awakened me. I looked to my right: my wife was sound asleep. I looked to the left at the digital clock; and to my complete surprise it was 4:44 a.m. *"Well now,"* I thought, *"this is certainly interesting."* And I slowly sat up in bed. Wow! What are the odds of that happening *twice in a row*? I stared at the clock and the red "4:44" seemed to be branding itself permanently onto my eyes. The room was very quiet, and I felt a bit out of place, not knowing what else I could do at this point. It was sort of like losing a bet, and not really knowing what you owed the other person. Feeling a little awkward, I laid back down and pulled the covers over me. My thoughts briefly returned to trying to figure out the odds of that happening by chance; hmmm...not likely. I'd done a considerable amount of gambling in my life—too much, in fact—and I certainly wouldn't have bet on that ever happening twice, even on a long shot. After a few minutes I fell back asleep.

In the morning, I sat on the edge of my bed and thought about what had happened during the night. For a moment, I considered telling my wife; and then voted against *that*. I wasn't sure that I'd be able to find any person who would even believe that you could—or even should—try to make a deal with God. And then, for me to tell them that I did, and that God actually participated, would seem quite far-fetched. They might end up doubting my sanity; so, nope! I'd first just have to think about all of this just a little bit more.

I should add, at this point, that I hadn't shared with anyone else this odd request I'd made of God; nor was I waking up at any other time during the night. I also found it intriguing, since I had given

God the choice of forty-four minutes after *any* hour, that He chose only 4:44 a.m.—as if to specifically make the point that it was *Him*.

During the days that followed, my work kept my mind totally occupied; and my nights were restful and uneventful. I was sleeping through the night without waking, and after a few days the whole matter of my "deal with God" was drifting and fading off as simply a fond and interesting memory.

"I was soon to find out that God had other plans.

Only an interesting memory? Thinking back, that may have been my idea; but I was soon to find out that God had other plans. He had given me plenty of time to respond in some fashion, and I obviously hadn't owned up to my end of the deal. In fact, I had failed miserably—and I was about to be confronted with the matter.

It was about a week since the last occurrence, and still nothing appeared to be out of the ordinary. I was sound asleep in bed when suddenly my eyes opened wide; again, something surely had awakened me. I looked to my right and saw that my wife was sound asleep. And now I hesitated. My mind was racing about what I might see if I turned around and looked at the clock. I felt as though I was being watched; and as I turned, it was like a child being caught by their parent with their hand in the cookie jar. It was, indeed, again 4:44 a.m! I could hardly believe my eyes. I was spellbound. Amazingly, what could only have been the holy, powerful and loving presence of God

started to fill my bedroom. My eyes started to fill with tears.

I didn't sit up. I couldn't have, even if I had tried; the powerful

presence of God in my room was overpowering. I could only roll out of bed and drop onto the floor. And then, for the first time as a grown man, I crawled up onto my knees, bowed my head, and wept. For someone so undeserving, I could never in my life have imagined the warm, loving embrace that followed. He truly was with me in my room.

CHAPTER TWELVE

The "Radio" Miracle

What I often refer to as my "radio miracle" actually involved the cassette player (radio system) in my red Datsun station wagon, and not a radio *per se*. This miracle happened in the year 2005, and I was at the time the Nova Scotia President of the (Federal) Christian Heritage Party of Canada (CHP).

Our CHP team in Nova Scotia had decided to host one of the quarterly CHP National Board meetings. This involved bringing in all the provincial presidents and the party's executives (fourteen members total) from all parts of Canada to Nova Scotia for a four-day event.

> "My downfall came as a result of becoming overtired by trying to oversee that all the activities were in place."

The preparations not only involved acquiring their accommodation and the venue for the meetings, but it also involved organizing some sightseeing events and a major banquet as a finale, prior to their departure. In the weeks and days leading up to the event, I had a small but excellent team to help me do some of the organizing and work; but anyone who has ever coordinated such types of events can well understand the magnitude of the workload involved. My downfall came as a result of becoming overtired by trying to oversee that all the activities were in place. I also tried to help coordinate those events during their visit, and simultaneously to be a responsible and active participant on the Board during the meetings. It goes without saying that our organizing team should have been larger, and I should have relinquished more of the control to the capable members of my team.

Left to right: CHP leader Ron Gray, banquet organizer Louise McKeen and author Jim Hnatiuk (looking very tired) one hour before miracle.

The two days leading up to the flight arrivals of the National Board members had me working flat-out, ensuring that everything was in place. When I finally was able to lie down to get a few hours' rest, my mind still wouldn't shut down, and that irritated me. Flight arrival of the Board members was on Wednesday; and when that day arrived, all the planned activities commenced. During the next two and a half days of Board meetings, I saw that all the planning was falling into place, while still trying to participate and contribute in the meetings as Nova Scotia President. By Friday afternoon of the last day, I was certainly looking forward to the banquet in Enfield that evening, prior to the Board's departure the following morning. I could see the end in sight.

Weeks later, I estimated that I'd had no more than four hours' sleep in just over four days. I obviously was not someone who should be driving a car, alone—at night.

The NS team had done an excellent job of organizing the banquet; it was well-received and well-attended. At the close of the event, those in charge of transportation saw to it that all the members of the Board were transported back to their accommodations in Debert, NS. The trip from Enfield to Debert would take about 45 minutes. I had to return some items from the banquet to my residence in Lantz, so I told the Board members I would meet them later that evening in Debert for refreshment, prior to us all retiring there for the evening. In the morning, I would assist in getting some of them to airport in Halifax for their scheduled flights home.

After everyone had departed, I loaded what I needed into the back of my Datsun wagon and dropped those things off at my home in Lantz. I told my wife I'd be sleeping in Debert and would see her in the morning after dropping a few members off at the airport. She told me to be careful driving, because she knew I was exhausted; and she even suggested I stay home and drive to Debert in the morning to pick up the members. I'd previously informed the board of my intentions to sleep in Debert, so I decided to follow through and make the remaining 40-minute trip.

> *"I...turned the volume down to a very low setting."*

It was approximately 11 p.m. as I made my way on the 102 Highway towards Truro, after which I'd turn in the direction of Debert. It was a bit cool outside, so prior to departing I had turned the heat on slightly to make it comfortable in the car.

I had popped in one of my favourite soft Christian music cassettes into the player and turned the volume down to a very low setting. The first 20 minutes of the trip was quiet, and there was very little traffic on the highway.

Maybe fittingly, that last thing I remember was passing the large green highway sign on my approach to Truro, announcing the "Bible Hill" turn-off. As nearly as I can tell, that was when I fell asleep at the wheel.

What could have only been seconds later, I was abruptly awakened by a sudden loud blast of music coming from my car's cassette player. The music was playing so loud! I'd never heard it so loud. At that instant, my head had bounced up, my eyes opened, and I wondered what in the world was happening! I straightened the car back into my lane, and within seconds it dawned on me that I had just fallen asleep. I immediately rolled down the window and let the cool night air rush into the car; *"Wow, what a close call,"* I thought.

Continuing to drive with my window wide open and the fresh air pouring in, my mind was trying to figure out just what had happened. Even after a kilometre or so, I didn't care that the music was still playing full blast—it was helping me stay awake, and I was grateful that it had awakened me in the first place. But why was the music so loud? How in the world did that happen? As I drove, I was perplexed, and wondered what on earth was going on.

After a minute or so of pondering these questions, I suddenly felt what could only be described as a momentary supernatural angelic presence with me in the car. I instantly understood that God had intervened to take care of me, and had sent an angel to turn up the music. I didn't see anything out of the ordinary inside or outside the car; I only felt this awesome presence around me, and being instilled with this message.

"I hardly ever take anything at face value."

As I drove along, my mind quickly started to analyze all this information. I hardly ever take anything at face value any more, and always find it necessary to decipher everything—especially something out of the norm, such as this. Because my expertise in the military was electronics, I understood in-depth how radios, cassette players, volume control circuitry and speakers operate; that was part and parcel of my trade. I understood the unlikeliness of circuitry malfunctions that could cause the music go to full volume; but even if it was a remote possibility, it couldn't be ruled out. That such a malfunction could be responsible for what had happened may not be out of the question; however, the timeliness of such a malfunction in this case could only have been a Godsend. I then suddenly realized that I could test to determine if it was a circuitry malfunction, or if in fact an angel had actually turned the knob to increase the volume of the music.

As I drove along with the music still playing full blast, I started to glance back and forth at the volume control knob on my cassette recorder. That knob, I knew, was the only way to control the volume; and when I inserted the cassette after leaving home, I distinctly remembered having turned the knob down to a very low setting so that the music played very softly. So if in fact an angel had turned up the volume, that would mean the knob should now be at maximum, and not at a low setting. I also understood that a malfunction in volume control circuitry could not cause the knob to turn on its own. That's not possible! With the music still playing full blast, I decided I would check to see what the position of the knob was.

Finally mustering up the courage to reach over, I grasp the knob and I started to turn down the music; Incredibly, I had to turn the knob almost a full turn before the music was down to a comfortable level. I realized then that the knob had, in fact, been turned up to full blast. I also knew I didn't do it, nor could it have been a malfunction.

At this realization, I was almost in tears because of what God had done for me. I'd been able to prove to my doubting mind that something supernatural did, indeed, turn that knob!

CHAPTER THIRTEEN

The Greatest Miracle

Before I share a few other mini-miracles—out of my list of many—I'll share with you what I refer to as the greatest miracle in my life, to date.

About the year 1996, a year or so after I retired from the navy, the most significant event in my life thus far took place. At this time I was about three years into my new thirst for knowledge about God. It was only after I had read so many factual books, and also what other authors had to say on the subject of God, that I decided to start seriously reading sections of the Bible for myself.

"My nature was such—a skeptic." My nature was such—a skeptic— and because of the claims of the Bible, I felt that what the Bible stated should be expected to stand at face value. In other words, if the Bible dared to make bold statements and claimed them to be true, then I felt that I had the right to be equally bold and challenge God to own up to that what is written in the Bible.

I'll be quoting some of the statements in the Bible with which I had real issues, so it's important that I show you where in the Bible I found those statements. You should know that each major segment of the Bible is called a "book," and each book has a name; then each chapter in that book has a number; and each verse in each chapter has a number. So I can easily identify the places where you can find my references, just in case you happen to have a Bible and want to check out what I'm claiming.

In 2 Timothy 3:16, it says that God inspired the different authors of the Bible to write what they did. When I read that, I figured, "That's just great; if God told them what to write, then everything in the Bible must be true, right?" OK; that's when I figured I'd soon be checking out to see if that was true.

A goal of mine was also to find out if someone could actually get closer to God. Was that just a myth, or simply an inner sense or feeling that some people claim to have had? Was it really just emotionalism? Also, is that literally what the Bible was stating or talking about? Just how close can you get to God if you are still alive and in this world?

"Just how close can you get to God?"

As you might expect, I was very pleased to find in the Bible where it states: *"Draw near to God, and he will draw near to you"* (James 4:8). "Really!" I thought. "Well that's just great, isn't it? If God had the author write that, it must be true, right? So let's see if that's possible."

I knew that I was going to be very skeptical and difficult to ever be convinced on this matter; but nevertheless, my outside research up to this point was fairly convincing that God was real, so I was open to trying to get closer—if only I could figure out how.

Some of the things I was reading in the Bible were starting to sit uneasy with me; yet at the same time it was sort of exciting. Especially when one day I read that anyone with a pure heart will be able to see God. I thought, *"Really? See God?"* Yes, that's what it said. If you look in the book of Matthew, chapter 5 and verse 8, it says: *"Blessed are the pure in heart, for they will see God"*. Well, when I read that Scripture, it really stuck with me!

"This is exactly what I was looking for," I thought. Reading further in James 4:8 (quoted above), it goes on to say, *"Draw near to God, and he will draw near to you...purify your hearts."* There it was again, about having a pure heart. I decided that this was my opportunity; I would take that scripture verse and test to see if this was, in fact, true.

> *"I decided I would focus solely on that one Scripture."*

At the time, I was living with my family in our very nice split-entry home on Highway 2 in Lantz, NS. Please understand that over the previous three years of study, my embarrassment about praying (even privately) had diminished substantially. So I had no problem now to start asking God to prove to me that the Scripture was true. Almost every day and evening, I would devote some special time to praying to God, asking Him to own up to what it said in Matthew 5:8. I decided I would focus solely on that one Scripture, and be persistent.

Be assured, I was very dedicated to the task of praying for this to be realized; but after a couple of months with no results, I was getting frustrated; nothing was happening. So I found myself arguing with God: "Why am I not allowed to see You? Surely my heart is pure and sincere enough?" This was the way I approached my discussions with God; and I know this process and reasoning may sound a bit crude to some Christians, and maybe even to non-Christians; but I can assure you that my heart and sincerity at the time were certainly 100 percent behind this, and certainly God would know that.

After that two months, I decided to give up on that particular prayer; but before I abandoned the endeavour completely, I started asking God to tell me or show me why He did not own up to what the Scripture claimed: "You told the authors what to write, God. So why haven't I been able to see You?"

Wow! That prayer had results almost immediately. During prayer time, I often took a couple of minutes to become quiet and simply listen. It was during one of those times that suddenly, and very clearly, someone, somehow, spoke to my mind (inaudibly) to say: *"Jim, you don't have a pure heart."*

Say what? I don't have a pure heart?! Wow! It was like a light came on in a dark room. I didn't have a pure heart? I certainly didn't expect *that* answer. If that's the case, what in the world does a person have to do to have this "pure heart" the Bible is referring to? Even though I didn't like the answer, I was encouraged by at least having received an answer; so I immediately changed my prayer. I now was praying: "Give me a pure heart. Show me what I have to do to have a pure heart, God."

"Why all these problems?"

I persisted for weeks. As the weeks passed, I transitioned into a season where some situations in my life were becoming very difficult. Numerous problems arose that were overly challenging. I had pretty much forgotten about my quest to see what was written in Matthew 5:8 realized, because I was now preoccupied by the turmoil I was undergoing. I would no sooner have one people-problem under control than another would surface. This went on for a few months, and I soon realized that my situation had gone from pretty good to becoming a near-disaster. My regular prayers had gone by the wayside, because I was dealing with all these issues. Frustrated by this avalanche of issues, I decided to call on God again to help me out of them. I returned to some regular prayers, and called out to ask Him why all this turmoil was happening to me. Wasn't I being a faithful person? Why all these problems? Do I deserve this? It's interesting to note here that it always seemed to take an escalation of adversity in my life to cause me to return to seeking God.

Well, it wasn't long before I got my answer to that prayer; and once again, I was shocked to hear it: *"I'm putting your heart to the test, and in that way allowing you to see the condition of your heart. I'm answering your prayer."*

I could hardly believe it. In order to answer my prayer, He was putting me to the test? Couldn't He just tell me what to do, and save me the pain? He was making me deal with these problems to find my own answer? All this hardship because I had innocently prayed: "Give me a pure heart, show me what I have to do to have a pure heart, God."

Yes, that's exactly what He was doing. We all know that reading a book about something, or someone giving you the answer to a question, does not necessarily produce lasting results; but having to live through the experience is when true transformation and revelation can take place. Experience it first hand, and you'll remember it and learn from it forever.

So yes, that barrage of people-problems I'd experienced over that few months was something I had brought on myself. God had me deal with them so that He could open my eyes, and I could then see just how impure my heart really was; and in that way I'd know what I needed to do to purify it. That was certainly a major revelation; and also a bit humiliating. I embarrassingly had to admit that I'd have to do a better job of dealing with such people-problems in the future.

I also made a mental note that I'd certainly have to watch what I prayed for in the future....

I'll spare you the details of each of those individual problems that I was forced to deal with over those couple of months, as each would probably require another chapter; and really, their subject matter is not the point here. It's sufficient to say they all dealt with and impacted my feelings towards others, and how I related to solving these situations with or without a pure heart.

The true character of a person comes out when they are put under pressure, and I was directed to read Matthew 15:18 which reminded me that I'd be able to tell what was in my heart by what came out of my mouth.

It was certainly a wake-up call for me, and a time to humble myself. I could much better understand, now, what it meant to have a pure heart in the situations I had been confronted with, and what I'd have to do, going forward, to correct my ways, my thinking, my attitudes, and my approach to issues.

So what now? Having now gone through those tough trials, I figured I might as well try to capitalize on them. I mean, I had unknowingly inflicted that process on myself in order to see Matthew 5:8 realized: *"Blessed are the pure in heart for they will see God"*—so I might as well follow through to see what I could gain from this, now that I figured the hard part was done.

I returned to regular prayer and thanked God for the process he had initiated to expose and clean up my heart. I returned to my request to see God—to have a close encounter with God, to have whatever Matthew 5:8 means, happen to me. I even dared to asked God if my heart had been sufficiently dealt with.

"Then...unannounced —it happened."

And then a few days later, unannounced—it happened.

It was in the morning; I was the first one up and decided to enjoy a coffee out on the patio. It was sunny and warm; late spring, birds singing and the dew still on the grass. As I stood overlooking the backyard, everything smelled so fresh; and then something started to happen that was definitely different: I noticed that the green in the leaves had much more depth, more colour, like a deep "living" green (if there is such a colour). I could see drops of dew hanging on the leaves up to fifteen or twenty yards away, each emitting the beautiful colours of the rainbow. Wow! At that distance, they looked like little diamonds! Everything in my backyard was increasingly becoming much more beautiful and pleasant; it was as if my eyes and ears had been given new, incredible power—and then, without any warning or request on my part I was suddenly "*taken*" in the "spirit." Yes, you heard me right! There was no travel time—it happened in the twinkling of an eye; it was instantaneous. My spirit left my body. In fact, it left the planet!

"I was awe-struck by such a wonderful experience."

I was taken to a place that had me hovering over what appeared to be the rough surface of the moon. I was looking directly towards planet earth, and it was absolutely astounding and astonishing. I saw what you'd expect the astronauts would have seen on their trip to the moon. I was actually there: I was hovering over the barren surface of what could only have been the moon. I was not on it, but about fifty feet above it. The earth was in full view in front of me; it was

This is a recreation of what Jim's location looked like.

huge, and rotated very slowly. It was absolutely breath-taking. I was awe-struck by such a wonderful experience. I felt "larger" and freer in the spirit; my senses were much sharper, my vision much clearer. I was neither afraid nor alarmed.

But it got much, much better than this. The most incredible part of the experience was not what was in front of me, but rather what was behind me. I

> *"His absolute power was penetrating, and He had intelligence unfathomable."*

didn't have to turn around (as strange as that might sound). I could actually *see* (or sense) without looking with my eyes. What was behind me was the most incredible, powerful and unimaginable "living" presence! His absolute power was penetrating, and He had intelligence unfathomable. How I was able to appreciate the level of His intelligence and feel His power is beyond me; it simply permeated every part of me.

Nothing could ever stand against or challenge what was behind me. Such a powerful "living presence" is something unheard of and unimagined on earth. It's difficult to explain, because there is nothing to compare it to; it was a perfect combination of *power* and *intelligence* immersed and transmitted by *love* from its core to its outermost extremities.

His *presence* would bring even the most evil and vile thing to its knees in tears. In a war, even amidst a full-out battle, His presence coming on the scene would have the greatest armies on earth immediately stop their attacks against each other, and instead fall down and worship Him. It's a presence you would rush to and want to bask in and take refuge in forever. His size (if it had dimension) was enormous.

Try to imagine a mountain a hundred miles high, a hundred miles wide and a hundred miles deep. Imagine that

somehow such a huge mountain was instead a "Living Being"—
an incomprehensibly tangible, penetrating, powerful and all-
intelligent *love*. A love not yet experienced nor understood on
this earth, breathtakingly powerful. This love had immense
unimaginable power, unlike the love we know on earth that
most often leaves us vulnerable. Spending a few thousand years
just basking in the presence of this love would go by far too
quickly. A remnant of His presence near the earth would
cleanse the world of every evil. The breeze coming off the
movement of His little finger would be felt by an entire community,
and transform anything evil to become good.

Besides being totally engulfed and saturated within this presence, I could feel this love very deeply and powerfully beating, as
would a heartbeat, penetrating through every part of me.

Yes, my most powerful, indescribable heavenly Father stood
directly behind me, lovingly showing me what He had created:
The earth, in all its splendour, in front of me—that I could see
with my eyes.

God, in all his majesty, was proving to me, in the most
incredible way, that He was true to His Word. *"Blessed are the
pure in heart, for they shall see God."*

THE RETURN TRIP

Then, as unexpectedly as I had departed, I was instantaneously returned into my body. I was back on the patio with my
coffee still in my hand. I'm not sure of how long I was *"taken,"* but
it could have been as long as two or three minutes. I stood there
on my patio in wonderment, wishing I hadn't returned. I looked
around. My coffee hadn't spilled, and I sort of wondered what my
body was doing during the time my spirit had departed—especially
as I had been standing, holding a cup of coffee.

I contemplated for days the enormity of what had happened, without sharing it with anyone else. Would anyone even believe me if I decided to tell them? My goodness, was this something else I'd have to keep secret?

Then it happened again.

"It happened again."

The exact same experience (journey) happened again about two weeks later. The second time it was again in the morning, and this time I was enjoying a coffee downstairs in our rec room. I had just sat down and was contemplating turning on the TV to watch the news. On this occasion, as well, I was *"taken"* without notice or announcement of any kind. I was not praying at the time, nor do I remember even being particularly God-conscious at the time. Again, it was instantaneous—there was no travel time; it was every bit as powerful as the first encounter and lasted approximately the same amount of time.

Why the second trip? My sense was that God provided this second encounter as an extra assurance, because He knew I was a skeptic; and just like I was with the 4:44 miracle, He'd make sure that even over time, I'd never doubt or forget what had happened. I'd also remember more clearly how to describe it.

Over the months and years that followed, I never felt that I was required to share these experiences. On the other hand, I never felt that I was being told to hide them, either. However, over the years, I did eventually share them with a few close friends and a few pastors. I knew that when God wanted me to share them with the world, He'd let me know. In the meantime, they'd become my very own "living source" of encouragement and assurance, each and every day.

CHAPTER FOURTEEN

Mini-Miracles

> *"By calling them mini-miracles, I don't want to belittle their significance or my gratitude for them."*

I've shared with you what I would consider to be the three most powerful miracles that have happened in my life to date. However, I've had, and continue to receive, untold others that I often refer to as mini-miracles—some of which are, in fact, actual genuine and explicit answers to prayers. By calling them mini-miracles, I don't want to belittle their significance or my gratitude for them. As I see it, my Father in heaven gives me big gifts and small gifts, much like our earthly parents would do. These mini-miracles (some answers to prayers) being thrown into my day-to-day activities certainly make my life interesting and enjoyable. They also serve to remind me of how close God remains alongside me; that He protects me and continues to provide even the smallest of things for me. That is not to say that He doesn't continue to teach me through various means; He certainly does.

As you read through this selection of my so-called mini-miracles, you may tend to think that some of these occurrences were simply coincidences. Everyone I know has had what he or she may refer to as lucky coincidences; and they probably never think that God had anything to do with them. You know what? Maybe He didn't and maybe He did; that's not for me to judge. However, I'm not speaking about happenstance; I'm definitely referring to God-incidences, because in each of these cases and in His own way, He has reminded me that He was involved.

> "The ability to sense God's presence becomes unmistakable."

After a significant number of these occurrences happening (and continuing to happen) in my life, and that they happen with perfect timing and end with a perfect outcome, I can say with confidence they are without a doubt God-incidences. I have an advantage over some in saying this, because with every single occurrence I also experience a profound sense of God's presence around me at about the close of each incident. That's right! Each time a mini-miracle occurs, or shortly afterwards, I will experience a divine sense of God's presence (even if it's just for a few moments)—long enough and in such a way that I instantaneously realize that He was alongside, He was the initiator, and He wants me to know that He was there to help me. For those who have yet to experience God first-hand, please understand that the ability to sense God's presence becomes unmistakable, especially after being afforded my earlier powerful encounters I had had with Him.

Over the last fifteen years now, many times after a significant min-miracle occurred, I had taken the time to record what had happened. Each was profound enough to have me sit down and make a journal entry, so I could save the details for another day. Today, I'm able to review those notes and hand-pick just a few that I'll be sharing with you in this book. I say this so you understand that my list is long, and it continues to grow. I also share these encounters so you can get a sense of the relationship that I've come to experience and enjoy with God, and how we interact on a day-to-day level.

PAPER CLIPS, 1996

At first it started out that I was just annoyed; and then, after a few weeks, that elevated to being somewhat frustrated; whenever I needed a paper clip I simply couldn't find one! I was also continually forgetting to buy a box of them, every time I was in a store. Today, I needed three paper clips; and once again, after a considerable search through my home office, I could only come up with one. Sitting in my office chair, I rested my head in my hands and thought, *"How could I be so stupid as to once again not remember to get paper clips?"*

"God says he's interested in every aspect of our lives."

I don't think I was being unduly hard on myself, because this had been going on for over a month. Then a thought occurred to me: *"God says He's interested in every aspect of our lives; the Bible says He even has the hairs on our head numbered (Luke 12:7)."* So I teasingly figured, *"Let's give this little frustration over to God and see how He deals with it."* "Father in heaven, I need paper clips." With that short prayer, I went back to work and forgot about that short interruption in my day. I used the one paper clip I had found and simply piled the rest of my paperwork in order.

A little while later, I had to visit my bank in Elmsdale to make a deposit and pay a few bills; after which, it was my intention—if I could remember this time—to drop down to the pharmacy and pick up some paper clips.

I picked up the paperwork I had organized earlier, and headed off to the bank. Once I was in front of the bank teller, I told her I wanted to pay the bills I had with me, and I pushed the pile of papers over to her. As she was going through my bills to be paid, she removed the one paper clip I had had and set it aside. Once she was all finished, she smiled and asked me if I wanted my paper clip back. Thinking "*Waste not, want not,*" I said, "Sure, thank you."

On that note, she smiled again and asked me if I needed more paper clips. Amused, I answered, "Yes, I do." At that, she reached under her counter and pulled out a glass jar filled with paper clips. She said she collects them from all the other customers who leave them behind. She reached for a plastic bag and poured the entire contents of the jar into the bag and handed it to me. As she did that, I felt a hint of God's presence around me—and only long enough and strong enough to remind me that He was providing me with the paper clips I had asked of Him.

Walking out of the bank, I could hardly believe His timing; and I was simply amused at how He had it all unfold. God was interested in helping me with even the smallest and most ridiculous frustrations in my life. He'd answered my prayer in less than an hour, and He saw to it that it wouldn't cost me a dime. I thanked Him.

PISTACHIO, 1997

My wife Ellen and I were grocery shopping at Sobeys in Elmsdale one evening. I don't often shop for groceries; but sometimes I just enjoy tagging along, and this was one of those rare occasions. We started off in the fresh fruit section; and after a couple of minutes, we were passing by a shelf that contained an assortment of nuts. Both Ellen and I enjoy nuts of various types; but we especially love pistachio nuts, so I picked up a bag to check out the price. After showing the price to Ellen, she immediately said they were too expensive. I sadly had to agree, because I didn't have a clue what a good price would be anyway; so I hesitantly and reluctantly put the bag back on the self, and we moved on. Be it known that we only enjoyed eating pistachio nuts about once a year, simply because of their cost.

After about an hour, Ellen had completed her shopping; so we headed for the cashier and then home to Lantz with our groceries on board. As we were pulling into our driveway, both Ellen and I noticed something white attached to the doorknob of our garage door. On closer examination we could see that someone had visited our home during our short absence and, realizing that we were not home, they had left something in a white bag for us to find. We got out of the car, and I went over to find out what was in the bag. Upon opening the bag, I could see that there was two or three pounds of fresh pistachio nuts inside. That was twice as much as what we had hoped we could have bought earlier. It was hard to believe our good fortune, and there was no note as to who left the nuts.

"God reminded me that he appreciates a husband and wife coming to an agreement even over small things."

Later that evening, upon quiet reflection about the pistachio nuts, my thoughts came together to realize that God cares about what we desire: *"And those who commit their ways to the Lord are given the desires of their heart"* (Psalm 37:4). God reminded me that He appreciates a husband and wife coming to an agreement even over small things; that even though we hadn't prayed to have pistachios, *"He knows what we need, even before we ask Him"* (Matthew 6:8). In so doing He provided us with twice what we had hoped to buy in the first place—and at no charge. A treat both Ellen and I would enjoy. I thanked Him.

HOW DID THEY GET THERE?

You may be wondering if we ever found out how the pistachio nuts got put on our garage door. Yes we did; and let me share that with you.

Since I had retired from the military in 1995, I was at the time operating a couple of small part-time businesses out of my home in Lantz. One business was taxidermy, and I was mounting a number of animals for local customers. One customer was of Chinese descent, and this gentleman observed old-school Chinese traditions. One custom he observed was bringing us a gift each time he visited to do business. Yes, every time he visited us he would bring a different gift. One time he brought us two beautiful green table lamps—a perfect match to our bedroom décor; another time, a type of Chinese sweet treats; another time a traditional Chinese dish. I loved this custom, but was honestly embarrassed at times at having to accept these gifts. He was very generous.

The day Ellen and I were grocery shopping, he had come by while we were out to pick up some frozen black bear paws from which he allegedly made black bear soup. When he realized we weren't home, he left the customary gift he had chosen for us that day hanging on our doorknob. Pistachio nuts. Perfect timing!

ALPHA, 1997

A few years after my retirement, Ellen's best friend, Susan, told me about a program called Alpha. As it turned out, this popular ten-week program was developed in England by a former lawyer, now a pastor, Nicky Gumbel; and it  was now being offered worldwide. After some initial investigations on my part, I found it to be an excellent small-group program that introduced the Christian faith to people in a most remarkable, non-threatening and friendly way. I immediately asked the senior leadership of the church I was attending in Elmsdale about the feasibility of our church hosting one of these courses. I got the green light from our senior pastor (nicknamed Fozz), and that started my twelve-year passion in directing close to twenty courses, not only in that church, but also in numerous others.

> *"The requirement for the electronic splitter was critical for the evening going ahead."*

My nature is such that I'm very particular that everything be organized to the highest degree possible; and so it was for each evening of those ten-week courses. As many as fifty to seventy people would attend the regular Tuesday evening sessions, and the responsibility to see that everything went smoothly rested heavily on me as the director. It was on one of those evenings, and only thirty minutes or so prior to starting time, that the "splitter" for the video machine was found to be malfunctioning. Because it was the forty-minute video that provided the subject matter for the group discussion, the requirement for the electronic splitter was critical to the evening going ahead.

There I was, thirty minutes to show-time, in a conundrum, wondering where in the world I'd be able to find such an item at such short notice—and especially at that hour of the day. The small electronic store at the Elmsdale mall was closed, and travelling all the way to Dartmouth would take too long, and was therefore out of the question. I thought, *"I don't deserve this, God! After all, I'm trying to introduce people to You in the same way that I know You. So why can't things go a lot smoother?"*

Then the thought occurred to me: the Enfield Hardware Store did sell a few electronics, and they just might have such an item. It was worth a try. I made the seven-minute trip from

Elmsdale to Enfield, and hurriedly walked into the hardware store. Because I was in such a rush, I thought to save time I'd ask the first employee I could find; but as luck would have it the two I saw were busy with other customers. Darn the luck! I quickly started walking down the different aisles, carefully looking out for any area that might contain such an item. Almost completing the second aisle, I said, *"OK, God, it's You and me, and I can't afford to not find this item."*

Moments later, I distinctly heard someone in the next aisle over drop something on the floor. Hoping that it might be another employee, I turned the corner to have a look down that aisle. Hmmm...? Not a soul in sight. *That's strange; I know I heard something drop.*

I slowly walked down the aisle to the area where I thought I heard something drop. I was certainly perplexed as to how something could have dropped with no one around. The thought then actually occurred to me that maybe God got involved in my search, and had the needed item fall to the floor. Hmmm. A bit far-fetched; but I'd never rule it out. Wow, was that it? A little way off, I saw the item that had dropped, lying on the floor. Wishing in a crazy sort of way that God had it fall so I could find it, I wandered over to have a look. Nope, no luck, darn it; it was something else. I picked it up to see where it had fallen from, and could see that it had come off one of the lower hooks on the shelf. I knelt down to hang it back onto the hook it had fallen from, and once on my knees, directly in front of my face was hanging a single "electronic splitter"—the exact item I was looking for!

God not only got involved, He organized my finding the item in such a way that I'd be on my knees when I realized he had put the item right in front of me to find it. I was, of course, now in the proper position to thank Him—yes, on my knees. What a hoot! Not only was I thankful, but I chuckled all the way back to the church, amused at how God would take the time to orchestrate things down to such a detail when dealing with "me of little faith." His timing was perfect—as always.

MOOSE CHARGE, 1989

> *"A number of significant miracles did occur in my life that had me perplexed."*

Remarkably, even before my transition of faith, a number of significant miracles did occur in my life that had me perplexed. Let me share just one of those with you.

During my four-year posting to Saint John, NB as a navy Quality Assurance overseer for the building of our City Class destroyers, I had the opportunity often to go deer hunting in the area surrounding Hampton, where we lived at that time. On one such hunting trip, I parted ways with my hunting partner, Frank, to go on a lone hunt into an area that I thought might be promising. Because I'd never scouted that area before, I took a compass bearing and decided to walk what turned out to be about a one-half-kilometre track through unfamiliar territory, to check it out.

After about thirty minutes, I noticed that the terrain and foliage had changed somewhat. I found an old, grown-in surveyor's line that matched my compass heading, and I decided to walk along it for a spell. I wasn't long on this trail when I suddenly heard a few branches snapping off to my right; but I couldn't see what it was. It sounded like an animal running, about thirty metres from where I was. Because of the denseness of the small six- to seven-foot high evergreen trees that covered the entire area, my vision was very limited. I felt there was a good chance it was deer that had gotten wind of me, and would be soon long gone. Yes, I could definitely tell that something was running away; but to my surprise I could also hear something larger, running towards me. As the sound grew louder, being six feet tall, I strained to look over top of the trees to see what it might be; but it was difficult to see over the top of the little spruce trees that surrounded me. Finally, over the trees I started to see glimpses of a huge black hump of hair heading in my direction. It was the back of a very large animal, heading straight at me. My God! I suddenly realized that a cow moose was charging towards me because I had come too close to her and her two calves. The calves were running away, and their mother was coming to take me out.

My rifle, a 30/30 Marlin, suddenly felt totally inadequate; but I cocked it, nevertheless. Because of the thickness of the little evergreen trees, I realized I would only get a clear view of the moose when it would be about four to five metres in front of me—virtually at point blank range! The time to avoid or shoot an angry moose charging directly at you is *not* when it's only five metres from running you over! There was nowhere for me to run, nothing to climb, nor any place to hide. The terrain was flat, with scattered little evergreens; and I had now become the hunted, and was trapped into having to confront a charging moose!

The entire episode had taken less then fifteen seconds, and it was when the moose was only about five metres directly in front of me that it burst though the evergreen trees in a full charge. It was only then, when it finally broke into full view and we came eye to eye, that she amazingly came to an abrupt stop. Wow! Thank God! We were so close I could have almost reached out and poked her with my rifle. Even if I had tried to shoot her as she broke through the trees, she would still have had time to run me over.

"Phew! Wow! 'Thank You, God, for however You made her stop.'"

Face to face, we stared at each other for at least one long minute. She was breathing pretty heavily, and I could smell her, she was so close. Neither of us moved. I didn't want to alarm her; nor, at this point, did I think I had to shoot her. Finally, she made the first move: she turned around and walked off in the direction of her calves. Phew! Wow! *"Thank You, God, for however You made her stop."* I started breathing normally again.

I listened carefully to determine her direction of travel, and her distance from me. After about six or seven minutes, I estimated that she was well over fifty metres away, and well off to my right. I decided to continue down the surveyor's line, and in that way I'd soon have her and her calves well behind me. I hadn't travelled any more than about twenty metres when I heard crashing coming my way—oh, wow! The moose was once again charging towards me. My God! Once again, I had nowhere to run, hide or climb. The terrain hadn't changed; I was still among the small evergreen trees; so I was in the exact same predicament I'd been in only minutes ago! It was only seconds, and once again the charging moose broke out only a few metres directly in front of me, almost within touching distance. Astonishingly, the huge animal abruptly stopped again, almost like its legs had frozen. *"Thank You, God!"* She was breathing heavily, and her big eyes stared directly at me.

After about fifteen seconds of staring at each other, I softly spoke to her as I very carefully started to take a few steps backwards: "I mean no harm to your calves, and I'm going to go now." She watched me slowly depart, walking backwards; and when I was back far enough, I turned and quietly headed out of her territory under a new compass bearing.

I don't take for granted the favour and protection I was afforded that day. Cow moose protecting their calves have been known to trample and kill hunters, and have even been known to attack vehicles that get too close to their young ones.

SHOTGUN, 2007

About twelve years after my transition of faith and about eight months after I had officially established my new business, "Hnatiuk's Hunting and Fishing Ltd.," I was renting half the pottery building belonging to a lady named Dinamarca, next door to my home in Lantz, as I had prepared it to make my new store become a reality. I hired Doug, a trustworthy contractor who did a remarkable job to renovate the large pottery room into what then resembled a cozy hunting camp, and now had both a gun counter and fishing area for my customers.

The amount of shotguns and rifles I had in stock was largely restricted to my credit limit at distributors in Ontario. All too often, customers would ask me to order a gun for them because we didn't have it in stock. When these special orders came in, I would do everything to try and satisfy the customer. One such special order was a pump-style 20-gauge shotgun that had been ordered, and my customer was being very patient in waiting for its arrival. After more than a month of waiting—far too long—and numerous promises to my customer, the shotgun finally arrived.

"I quietly asked God why this was happening to me; I told Him that I was doing everything to run an honest business."

When I got to work the day the gun had arrived, Ron (an employee), who had opened and tested the action of the gun, told me the bad news: the shotgun didn't operate correctly; the pump action would continually jam. After close examination, Ron reported that a pin in the breech area was actually bent and out of place. What was so disappointing was that his only recommendation was that the gun would have to be returned to the distributor in Ontario. In desperation and disbelief, I asked him for the gun, so that I could see for myself. Sure enough, it malfunctioned just as he described. I lowered my head in disappointment, walked outside with the shotgun in my hand and sat down on the steps. I quietly asked God why this was happening to me; I told Him that I was doing everything to run an honest business and I wanted to satisfy my customers—especially this one, after him having to wait so long.

After a few seconds of having a private chat with God about my disappointment, I got up, preparing to walk back into my store. Just before turning to go back through the door, I decided to offer God the opportunity to fix the gun (or the situation), and so I quietly prayed for a few seconds or so over the gun. Then, not really expecting anything had happened, I tried operating the pump action on the gun again. What? It operated flawlessly! Was I mistaken? I tried it again: and it operated flawlessly again. Perplexed, I could hardly believe what was happening, and I immediately looked inside to view the pin that had been bent and out of place. It was perfectly in place. I pumped the gun repeatedly, fast and slow—and it operated perfectly. "Well look at that! You fixed the gun. Amazing!" I said.

With my chin held high, I walked back into the store and told Ron to call my customer to pick up his gun. Ron looked a little surprised, and when I handed him back the gun, he tried it himself—and was amazed that it operated flawlessly. Ron asked how I was able to fix it so quickly, being as how that pin had been bent. I told him that I didn't know how to fix it, so I asked God to fix it—and He did! I left it at that, and confidently walked out of the room.

JUST A TASTE

So by now I hope you're getting the idea of what I'm talking about. The reason for my sharing with you a few of the many mini-miracles I've experienced was to simply give you a taste or sense of what I have come to appreciate with God at my side. Most of these miracles, you could probably tell, I didn't expect to happen when they did. What's important to mention here is that I treasure each and every miracle; yes, they helped me—but more important: each one confirmed my ongoing relationship with my Father in heaven. Each time one occurs, I sense the closeness of my relationship with Him; and that's a powerful feeling and position to be in.

"Far too often, I pray for specific things and nothing appears to happen."

I honestly believe that these mini-miracles don't happen more often, simply because of my neglect, in not spending more private time with God and/or remembering to ask Him to intervene more often in situations I run into. Far too often, I pray for specific things and nothing appears to happen. This is foolishness on my part, because I know better, and it's something I obviously need to work at. I often wonder, with the rewards so great, what prevents me from spending much, much more time with God?

There are many other times, I'll admit, that I also recognize His fingerprints on my thought processes, or His handiwork on situations I'm dealing with or going through, even when I haven't specifically asked for help. Those come, I believe, as result of what I'd refer to as me being continually God conscious. I believe it's possible to achieve such a state of mind as being always aware that you are in the presence of God. It's *staying there* that takes commitment; but ultimately I know the rewards will be innumerable. That is, obviously, an area I'm currently working on.

Whenever I see anything ending perfectly, I'm always reminded of Who had to be involved and looking out for me. I really enjoy seeing His signature.

To go on now and expand on all the unique and wonderful mini-miracles I've recorded, plus those I can recall from memory, would be a book in itself. The main point here, that I hope you've come to appreciate, is that my life had definitely taken a complete one hundred and eighty degree turn, and had truly had gone from torments to miracles.

So how, exactly, could that possibly have happened? When and how did that transition actually take place? How was the tormentor finally defeated, and now replaced by such wonderful miracles?

CHAPTER FIFTEEN

The Transition Starts

How was it that I was able to bring to an end thirty years of torments, and move instead to a life filled with innumerable divine miracles and Godly encounters? How was this wonderful metamorphosis initiated? How was I able to finally rid myself of that deceptive tormentor, and start what I would refer to as leading a normal and exciting life—without those constant demonic interruptions?

"I can assure you that I had my share of negative religious experiences."

It's important to inform you, here, that in order for me to fully explain the transition out of those years of torment, some of what I write now may sound a bit far-fetched to the naked or virgin ear; but you have to know that what I write is true, so bear with me on this. I would also ask that you not let any former negative experiences you may have had with Christians or the Church deter you from reading what I will be sharing with you. I can assure you that I had my share of negative religious experiences; and because of them, you'd expect that I'd be one of the last to go back to that arena looking for solutions. In case you don't believe me, let me share one of those negative religious experiences with you.

"I share this so you'll know that I had every reason to distrust such organizations."

In Grade Nine, I was locked alone inside a chemistry lab at the Christian boarding school I was attending, and forcibly sexually assaulted by my male chemistry teacher. I'm not talking about a little touch here and there; it involved the teacher coming to an orgasm. I don't wish to divulge his denomination, so as not to discredit the religious order, because they were not responsible. It was a horrible and wrongful act against my person from an individual old clergyman, who obviously had problems of his own. To further the wound, even though I reported him to my school counsellor, nothing appeared to be done about it; and I was required to return the following year to that boarding school, and again required to sit in his chemistry classroom under his instruction for another full season. I share this so you'll know that I had every reason to distrust such organizations; and you'd expect that once old enough, I'd distance myself forever from so-called religion, church and/or god of any kind.

"I also know that God was not responsible for that old man's actions."

You can probably better understand, now, my hesitancy to involve the church in being a possible solution to my issues. But I also knew that God was not responsible for that old man's actions, nor today, do I hold any animosity towards him. Ultimately, as you're going to see, my solution involves God; but the solution I found *did not* come as a result of me starting to practice Christian traditions, i.e. going to church, tithing, reading the Bible, cleaning up my language, helping others, getting involved in church ministries, etc. *No*, it was not in those things that the real solution was found. You may be letting out a sigh of relief at this point, because I know many people I've met have already lost faith in those things. I know at the time, I was certainly one of them. I understand today that all those things have a place, a time and very good purpose; but they are certainly not the solution to which I'm alluding.

So what was truly the key? In all the religious teachings that were provided for me during my upbringing—and let me assure you, they were considerable—there was not one priest I can remember, not one pastor, not one Christian person, nor did any church material ever inform me of the fact that a very imperfect person such as myself could actually acquire a personal one-on-one relationship with God.

If this were true, and I've shown you that it is—if such a relationship is possible—how could so many in the church be forgetting to tell others about something so important as that? Is it because they feared that people might challenge them as to the depth of their own relationship? Is it because their own relationship with God was not one-on-one, and not really thought to be attainable to the level I have already described and I'm about to describe? Maybe some believed that all the other religious traditions had to be observed first, before such a relationship could be acquired. Or did they believe that only those who attained sainthood could have such a relationship—and surely not a sinner such as I was. Who can say? I only know that not one person ever took me aside and explained the importance of what I'm about to share with you and what you also can hope to achieve, if you so desire.

> *"I probably would have balked at such a suggestion, and certainly would not have taken the person seriously."*

Whatever the case may have been—and to be fair to that one forgotten person who may have tried to tell me—I probably would have balked at such a suggestion, and certainly would not have taken the person seriously. As you are probably well aware by now, no one could have been more wrong than I was—nor more pleased than I was to find myself wrong! Yes, I found the experience humbling; but once I saw the truth, I was easily able to swallow my pride—and that resulted in rewards that were out of this world! The question now is, are *you* able to swallow your pride? Reading my book to this point suggests that you may very well have the desire and stamina necessary to go the extra mile, to peek into the unknown, and dare to let it become known to you.

So what led me to that door, and convinced me to transition through it?

THE GREAT PURSUIT

My actual transition started in the early 1990s; and it was initiated, not by my quest to rid myself of the torments, but rather because I asked a friend a simple question about his faith. In that question, I wasn't seeking solutions for what plagued me all those years; I was just challenging a friend, because I figured I had a pretty good handle on religion. If you recall what I wrote earlier—and what cut like a knife— was how I was affected by Kenny's response: *"How can you love God with all of your mind, if you don't read and study to satisfy your mind?"*

The solution to ridding myself from years of torment and voices didn't come specifically as a result of my own probing into that matter. It didn't come as a result of my analyzing myself and trying to outwit the devil. Don't get me wrong—that continual exercise was still very important, because it prolonged my ability to withstand the devil over so many years. But the real solution, and what started my transition out of those tormenting years, would you believe, came as a by-product of me pursuing and going through the door that Kenny had opened for me.

> *"It was in that **great pursuit** that I also discovered the answers."*

Even though I had put on airs, claiming that I knew something about religion, I soon came to realize through study that I had really known very little. What had come as a complete surprise to me was the fact that it was not only permissible to question God, but that God Himself would help me find the answers. It was through and during my quest to seek a better understanding of God—and then (more important) realizing that I was able to acquire a closer relationship with God—that everything else started to fall into place. *It was in that **great pursuit** that I also discovered the answers as to how to deal with the tormenter.*

It's important that you also understand that when the demons realized what was happening, they immediately changed their tactics. They could obviously see that my quest for knowledge about the validity of God and the Bible was having positive results that they didn't want me to have; and therefore their strategy had to drastically change.

During the initial stages of my transition, it was hard for me to decipher exactly everything that was going on, as I was also caught up in the webs of new deceptions that the demons were unleashing to keep me off side. That was coupled (and combatted) with the effects that my prayers were having on the devil's long-standing tactics. I was experiencing a whirlwind of supernatural battles, but nevertheless, I was pleased by everything that was starting to happen. Let me explain.

> *"I started to believe that my prayers were, in fact, going to be effective."*

The off-again, on-again periodic torments started to fade, so much so that I started to make the connection. I came to realize that the more I studied and questioned God, the more answers I acquired; and so the higher my confidence and level of faith became. So it was that the more I sought to satisfy my mind about "this whole God thing," the more light bulbs came on; and as a result, I started to believe that my prayers were, in fact, going to be effective. Nor was I disappointed. The length of time between torments grew longer and longer; to the point when I realized that with concerted effort, I could actually pray those things out of my life. Wow! Was this actually happening? When I was exhausted through work, I could actually just relax and go to sleep without another battle to consider. This revelation encouraged me like no other.

"Previous to this, I had prayed, and at times I had prayed a lot; but those prayers had little to no results."

It's important to reiterate that it wasn't just because I was praying that resulted in the tormenter being arrested; *rather it was because my faith level was skyrocketing*—and my faith was growing at that incredible rate because of my pursuit of knowledge about God. Previous to this, I had prayed, and at times I had prayed a lot; but those prayers had little to no results, so I often abandoned the practice, and only came back to it when I was desperate. But because I was now questioning everything and finding answers that I never before knew existed, my faith was growing at an almost-incredible rate. If you recall what I wrote earlier, it was during those six months when I was questioning and studying every obstacle that stood in my way:

> *"Evolution, the speed of light, Adam and Eve, Noah's flood, scientific evidences, the hypocrisies in churches, so-called Christians, you name it, I couldn't seem to get my hands on enough books to satisfy my new thirst. Over the next six months to a year, my entire belief system was undergoing a major transition as I dove from one book to the next. As soon as my mind was satisfied enough on one subject, I'd immediately be driven to another."*

"*I trust you're starting to see the key.*"

So, as my mind was being satisfied, so was my faith level rising at an amazing rate; and the fact that God was becoming very real was not only intriguing, but also a sense of awe was starting to be established. I trust you're starting to see the *key* here: it was first my pursuit in trying to find out everything about God, my questioning everything that bothered me, and I mean *everything* (I even investigated the speed of light as it relates to an expanding universe at the time of creation); and then, because of the answers I was uncovering, my faith that God was indeed real grew from a foundation that originally could barely have supported only a house, to a foundation that now could support a skyscraper! When I simply had blind faith, and told people, "Sure, I believe that God is real," the effectiveness of my prayers to God carried that same blindness and uncertainty as did my faith in them. Praying to God with "skyscraper" type faith made all the difference in the world!

"*It wasn't my pursuit to find solutions to my problems that was key.*"

Lastly, allow me to remind you that it wasn't my pursuit to find solutions to *my problems* that was key: rather it was *my pursuit to find God* that became the solution to my problems.

It was during this season of growth that another strange but intriguing phenomenon entered my life. If you think for a minute, if you were that powerful enemy and saw my faith level escalating towards Godliness, what type of deception would you throw at me to try and derail me; what would you throw at me to have me abandon my quest for God? It would have to be pretty powerful, because my faith level was growing to skyscraper levels at an astonishing rate; and the devil would have to devise something pretty impressive to take me off track.

CHAPTER SIXTEEN

The Enemy's Tactic

"You will find this chapter to be one of the most difficult to believe."

In chapter 1 of this book I wrote: "*I'm sure you are going to find some of these amazing experiences very difficult to believe.*"

Well this is one of them. I'm confident that if you haven't already, you will find this chapter to be one of the most difficult to believe, because such things are thought by most to be impossible. Yet, because I have lived through the experience, with confidence I don't hesitate in sharing it with you. Regardless of what this might lead you to believe, and that I run the risk of it not being believed, it's more important you know then not know. Some have asked me if I happened to be on any kind of medication at the time. Fair question, but the answer is no, absolutely not. During this period of my life, I was a totally fit Chief Petty Officer working at one of my highest levels of performance. In fact, it was during this period of time that my performance evaluations gained me the scores I required for my promotion to CPO1.

That being said, allow me to endeavour.

I can't remember the first time it happened, but I do remember it had happened on a number of occasions before I started to wonder if I could make them happen by my own free

will. I wanted to make them happen, because I was really beginning to enjoy going on those excursions.

What I'm speaking about here is
"I didn't ask for this to happen, nor did I question why it was." commonly referred to as "astral projection," where your spirit or "astral" body
separates from the physical body, and
it's then capable of travelling outside
your physical body. I didn't ask for this
to happen, nor did I question why it was happening; it just started
happening "on its own," and I was enjoying it immensely. Having
my spirit outside of my physical body was certainly not uncommon
to me; but up to this point, it had always been a very terrifying
experience, and one that was used to torment me. Now, however, in
these new outings, I appeared to be in complete control as to where
I wanted my spirit to go and what I wanted to experience.

At first, when I realized I was outside my body, I limited
myself to just going for little strolls through my home to check
things out. While I was on these walks, everything appeared very
normal, and probably the same as if I were walking around in my
physical body. Only now, when I stood beside my wife or children,
they didn't know I was standing or sitting beside them. I found
that pretty incredible, empowering—and absolutely intriguing.

It was at work one day, when I was thinking about my last
out-of-body walk, and thinking about how cool it would be if I
could go over to visit the homes of some of my co-workers. I was
also wondering if any of them (or anyone else, for that matter)
was able to do the same thing with their spirit and body as I was.
I was certainly not going to ask them (for obvious reasons); but I
thought that if the next time I was outside my body, I visited their
home, I may find them doing their own out-of-body walks; and
then we'd get to know each other that way, an in-the-spirit relationship *per se*. My mind started to play with the possibilities of

having another whole life, separate from my regular life—a life just in the spirit. *"Wow!"* I thought, *"what an interesting concept!"* However, it wouldn't be much of a life if I couldn't find someone else with the same ability as me.

"Everything was fascinating and exciting."

With concentrated effort and a sense of adventure, I finally took the plunge to venture outside of my own home while I was on one of these out-of-body spirit walks. I was able to quickly teach myself how to dart (float) from one place to another simply by willing myself to be wherever I wanted to go. Everything was fascinating and exciting, and I started to make a few visits to other homes. I was able to see and mingle with some selected co-workers at their homes; but the frustrating part was not being able to communicate with anyone. No one else was walking in "the spirit," so no one else even knew I was around. My objective was not at all to peek into the affairs of my friends, but solely to find someone else who had the capacity to operate in the spirit like I was able to do.

At first, I had no clue as to when I might find myself on these out-of-body walks; they periodically just seemed to happen. But after a few months, I started to pick up on the pattern that allowed me to exit my body. Because of that, I was able to figure it out, and eventually felt that I could initiate when I wanted to go on such a walk, and how to make that happen by my own free will.

So, in the middle of the afternoon one day, I told my wife that I was going to lie down to rest for a while, and I did this so that I wouldn't be disturbed. I walked into the bedroom, closed the door and laid down on the bed. I closed my eyes and focused on leaving my body. Immediately, the familiar tingling sensation started to happen—and so rapidly that it totally engulfed my whole body in a matter of seconds; and the next thing I knew, I was able to float right out of my body, and then look back at my body still lying on the bed. I didn't have to walk; I could "float" at will to move around. My senses were keen; I fully understood that I had purposely just left my body to go for a "spirit" walk. I remembered that I had just told my wife not to disturb me—in other words my spirit mind was still fully cognizant of everything else going on in my life, and in full operation without my actual brain.

After a little walk around the inside of my house, I was happy with the fact that I was able to initiate the out-of-body experience myself. Now I had to see how well I'd do on the return trip back into my body. You should know that I didn't have to open doors; I could simply pass right through them.

> "My mind would re-enter my brain; and within seconds, my brain would come to life and take over the thinking."

I floated back into the bedroom, and found it easy to simply re-enter my body that was lying on the bed. With my spirit now situated within my body, I then concentrated on having my body come back to life by my spirit re-engaging with it. Immediately, I started to feel a tingle all over my body. This would happen now with very little effort. My mind would re-enter my brain; and within seconds, my brain would come to life and take over the thinking or start helping with the thinking process.

I could never totally understand what took place in that transition between my mind and my brain; but they came back to working in unison with ease. The coming back into my body had some similarities to the process that happened when I was trying to escape from the torturous times—those times when I was trapped inside my corpse and being terrorized. But now everything cooperated, everything happened at will: my body cooperated, and with very little effort on my part. Everything was enjoyable, captivating—and like an incredible new adventure.

Now that I understood how much I was in control of this phenomenon, I realized that having this ability was absolutely amazing! Over the next few months, I initiated numerous excursions to experiment with what I was able to do with this new power. My attempts to find more information on its origin, or read about others who may have this ability, were aggravated by the fact that I could find so little detailed information on it. The Internet world was just becoming a part of my life, so I didn't yet have that to assist me.

"This was like a dream come true."

My mind started to conjure up all kinds of ideas of how I might be able to capitalize on having such an unusual ability, that no one else I knew of (to date) had, but myself. My thinking started to race with all kinds of crazy ideas of how I could possibly use it: to make money; getting inside information on gambling; getting involved in having another whole family, a new "spirit" family. Wow! Would that be classified as adultery? Maybe probing into valuable information, and use it in the natural to better my life, or even to help the military, help my country. This was like a dream come true; I was virtually able to become "the invisible man" whenever I wanted to, and live another life, unknown to anyone else! Ultimately, I started to see this as a position of great power; but I was yet to figure out what I would actually do with it.

At the same time that all of this was happening, in the natural world you'll recall that I was in the middle of those six months when I was questioning and studying everything I could about God, and that my faith level was skyrocketing. Because of that, I was entertaining the thought that maybe I was being rewarded, and God was giving me this power. After all, who else would have the ability to give me such power?

All my efforts to try to find another person—or should I say, the "spirit of a person" on a similar "out-of-body" walk as me—didn't materialize. I found that even though I mingled among many people, they were all in the natural world, and no one else had this ability to be "in the spirit." I was alone, even though people surrounded me. I guess my question about the legitimacy of getting involved with another woman "in the spirit" wouldn't have to be put to the test, because there wasn't one to be found, anyway. Then the thought occurred to me: should I even be having these thoughts? If God had given me this power, surely I shouldn't be mixing in thoughts about "spirit" adultery, or gambling, or dishonesty. Even though I was thinking about the many good and great things I could do with this power, my thoughts also included some nasty things. Some red flags about this whole experience started to pop up in my mind. Why was it I had this ability and no one else appeared to have it? This ability was not only intriguing and perplexing, but also one that gave me a sense of much power.

"Was I being deceived big time?" At the height of my excitement a sneaky suspicion entered my mind that the devil might have returned under another disguise. Was the master deceiver, "the prince of darkness," up to this? Was I being deceived big time? I suddenly became very suspicious, and at the same time very disappointed in having to think that this could all be the work the devil himself. I knew almost immediately that I would have to put these out-of-body walks to the test, and try to find out who the provider was.

Reluctantly, I started putting everything that was happening into new perspective. If this was demonic, he wasn't showing his horns and tormenting me this time; but rather, he'd come back as the "angel of light." Had he found, in me, a willing and unsus-pecting subject? Gee, not again! These possible conclusions were so disappointing, because that possibility certainly existed. Even with all the good that I felt I could do with this power, there appeared to be evil embedded as a component to it. What was it that caused me to suspect that? It was because it was seducing me with untold powers that could lead eventually to things like, gambling, blackmail, and adultery. *That's* what made me suspect it.

Yes, when I analyzed my recent excitement about having this power, and I put my thoughts about it into honest perspective, I had to admit to myself that I was also contemplating doing nasty things, regardless of the good for which I knew I could use it. Very disappointed at the possibility of this assessment being true, I thought, *"Damn it to hell—the devil just may be behind this whole new out-of-body experience!"* So to be able to live with myself, I made the very difficult decision to test this phenomenon; if I found that the devil wasn't involved, nothing lost; but I figured I'd rather be safe than sorry. I also realized that if the devil were up to this, I would have to keep my suspicions secret from him so he wouldn't foul up my testing. The battlefield of the mind was nothing new to me; if the devil knew I was suspecting him, and if he knew that I was testing to see if it were he, he'd ensure my testing would fail, in order to have me believe he was *not* involved.

"Over the past thirty years, I'd learned that the devil had enormous power.

I thought about what my plan should be, to test what was happening to me. Because of what the Bible said, I under-stood very well that the devil is a liar and the master deceiver. So I figured that if he were involved in my out-of-body walks, I should be able to discover something deceptive—a lie about what was going on during my walks. After all, looking back to when I was being tormented by the devil over the past thirty years, I'd learned that the devil had enormous power. To scare me half to death, yes; but he was also able to actually create regular people, or monsters out of thin air—even situations, places, sounds, and smells; and he was able to put me into the middle of those scenarios, and have me believe they were actually happening to me. He was able to have me remember just what he wanted me to remember: for example, he was able to totally erase from my memory the fact that I had been tormented and fooled the day before. It's impossible not to fall prey to such incredible powers of deception. When those things were happening, I had to believe that they were in fact happening, because in fact they were very real—more real than life itself.

Because of those years of torment, and what I learned about the power of the devil to deceive, I was coming to the conclusion that what I was seeing and experiencing during my "spirit" walks might not all be true. Was the enemy creating life-like scenarios, creating people and situations that were in fact lies? *"Damn it!"* I thought. I was disappointed that these powers might not be God-related but actually demon-related.

"*I loved having this power.*"

As much as I disliked the idea of testing it, because I loved having this power, after some careful thought I came up with a plan that I knew I had to go ahead with.

In order to test one of my out-of-body walks, I decided to involve my wife without telling her ahead of time. I couldn't tell her, because if I did, the devil might hear me explain it to her, and therefore know what I was up to. If it was the devil, and he knew I was going to test the legitimacy of my experience, he'd make sure that I wouldn't be able to catch him deceiving me.

The way I decided my plan would work would be that Ellen would simply be my eyewitness to what was happening in the natural world, while I would observe what was happening when I was on a "spirit" walk around the inside of my home near my wife.

I was living at the time in our home on Highway 2 in Lantz. It was mid-afternoon, and I saw that Ellen was preparing something in the kitchen. My daughter Carlleen was in the rec room downstairs, and my son Doug wasn't home. I felt this was as a good time as any to give my plan a try. I hurried into my bedroom to lie down, and in less than a minute I was out of my body and in the spirit, floating down the hallway toward the kitchen. I noticed that Carlleen had come upstairs and was now sitting in the living room. Ellen was still in the kitchen preparing a meal, just as I had left her a minute earlier. I heard Ellen saying something to Carlleen, and then Carlleen responding. After I observed a few comments between them, I immediately returned to the bedroom to re-enter my body. Back in my normal state, I immediately walked to the kitchen; and as I entered, I couldn't see Carlleen in the living room. I asked Ellen if she had just been speaking to Carlleen, and she said, "No." I said, "Are you sure? Wasn't she just here in the living room speaking to you?" Ellen said, "No, she wasn't." "*Damn-it-to-hell!*" I thought. I realized, then, that I was right. I had my answer: this *was* demonic power, and he was mixing in what was real with what was his own fabrication. The devil could simply create people and conversations that were not even happening in the natural state, even though you'd bet your life that they had happened, because you had just witnessed it first-hand. I was very disappointed.

> "*The devil could throw a lie in wherever he wanted.*"

I knew from that time forward that I couldn't believe *anything* that was happening during these out-of-body walks. The devil could throw a lie in wherever he wanted. He had just fabricated Carlleen being upstairs and having a conversation with her mother, and if I didn't know better, I would have bet my life that that had actually happened. How dangerous was that? So much for helping my country with information-gathering, or betting real money on inside information. The devil is a liar.

Since the master deceiver was allowing me to have these experiences, I could be assured that his long-term plan was to eventually harm me and/or my family in their usage. With this so-called wonderful power—that I thought I was in complete control of—I was actually being slowly suckered-in for another major demonic experience down the road. These *spirit walks* were a part of another incredible setup, and I needed them to stop *immediately*. So I stopped my voluntary "spirit walks"; I simply decided to just stop doing them. I was still concerned about my involuntary walks—the ones that had introduced me to this whole experience in the first place. I decided to take those ones to prayer, and I was happy that God answered my prayer immediately: the involuntary "spirit walks" ceased; it was with my blessing that God arrested that demonic power. I thank God today that I haven't had an "astral projection" or so-called "spirit-walk" for over twenty years now.

> "Why had he reverted to giving me this power, instead of his usual torment?"

So what had the devil been up to? And why had he reverted to giving me this power, instead of his usual torment? I believe he became very concerned about me acquiring all that new knowledge about God. He could see where my life was going, so he came onto me with a brand new, powerful tactic to win me over, in an attempt to take me off-track from my investigations about God. Instead of tormenting me, he decided to give me what I thought was a wonderful and unique power. It almost worked, because the "spirit walks" had me, at one point, feeling totally awestruck about myself; and the fact that the torments had ceased was, to me, a miracle in itself. Why wouldn't someone suck that right up? True to the devil's plan, during that period I was starting to shift my entire focus more onto those powerful experiences that the devil had given me, than on my in-depth God investigations.

I have to thank God for the intuition and insight He gave me to test the spirit, and for helping me be rid of that deception. To conclude this matter, I'll add again that, "the prince of darkness" had effectively come to me disguised as an "angel of light"; and I can see how his powerful ability to sucker someone in has to be like child's play for him. It was only having God at my side that provided me my opportunity to escape that trap. I shudder to think of where that was all leading.

> *"I truly loved the power I thought I had been given; it was captivating, and I would never have wanted it to end."*

To conclude this matter, I'd like you to understand that the most intense struggle for me was deciding to test something with which I was infatuated. I truly loved the power I thought I had been given; it was captivating, and I would never have wanted it to end. So deciding to test it was painful; because in doing so, I realized that I might have to relinquish it. So it is with the things the devil is able to offer you, and hence the reason entrapment is like child's play for him.

One last thing before I close this chapter. In an earlier chapter, I reported on how that *little bag* which contained that miniature Gideon's Bible had appeared to all of a sudden lose its power. It was around the same time that I had uncovered the truth about those "spirit-walks" that I also found out the truth of why that *little bag* had lost its power when it did.

It happened that I needed a Bible for a quick reference one evening after going to bed; and not having one at my bedside, I remembered that I had some time ago thrown the *"little bag"* containing the miniature Gideon's Bible into the drawer of my bedside table. If you recall, I had stopped using it, because it was failing to stop the torments. Well, this particular night, I needed a Bible for reference, and thought it would save me having to get out of bed to go and fetch a larger Bible. So I opened the drawer, pulled out the little bag, opened it, and pulled out what I thought would be the miniature Bible I had put in it. What I found in there was certainly not a Bible. Someone, as a silly joke, had replaced my little Bible with a deck of dirty playing cards. Each playing card had pornographic pictures of naked women. No wonder the contents of the *little bag* had lost its power! In order to disarm me, the devil had effectively been able to find a willing subject, probably a shipmate, to play a joke on me; and as a result that little bag could no longer protect me each time I laid down to rest.

CHAPTER SEVENTEEN

Cleaning Up

It was two years prior to me retiring from the navy—which was about one year into all my study and investigations about God—that the key turning point in my life occurred. During that season of my life, I did something, really innocently, that triggered the cocoon to break open and allow my astonishing metamorphosis to be birthed.

At that time, my drinking parties (or binges) had become far and few between; I was trying my best to end them, and I would go as much as four to five months without abusing alcohol—and be quite proud of myself. But still, on rare occasions, I would fall into the trap of drinking too much—even after I had promised myself that I would never do that again. It was especially on those rare occasions I'd regret like hell having to live the next three days trying to get the effects of the alcohol out of my life, and my body back into shape. I found those mornings, however few, horrible; because regardless of the length of time since my last binge, an evening of over-drinking would invariably result in a blackout the next morning. I had to then rely on others to inform me how "good" a time I'd had the evening before. Most disappointing was being reminded by the look in my wife's eyes that she didn't appreciate just how good a time I'd had.

> "I was still trying to correct things my way, which was the only way I knew how."

It's important to remind you that even though I was totally engulfed in my study about God, and had been for about a year; and even though my faith level was growing amazingly, I was still finding it hard to get my life on a proper track. I was still (regrettably) misbehaving from time to time—and I was about to find out why: it was because *I* was still in control; I was still trying to correct things my way, which was the only way I knew how.

So yes, it was as a result of me finding myself once again suffering through one of those terrible mornings; I found it so humiliating that I had to look up for help. I distinctly remember sitting on a small bench in my backyard that Sunday morning, nursing my hangover headache with a glass of wine, and afraid of finding out about the stupid things I may have done the night before—things I'm sure Ellen would soon be reminding me of when I went back into the house. This particular morning, my greatest regret was specifically over my stupidity and weakness in finding myself once again in this situation. I had promised myself so many times that the previous time would be my last time— only to find that here I was again. I was frustrated: *"My God, I just can't take having to live through these horrible mornings any more!"* I was truly fed up with myself. I felt angry at not being able to completely quit this foolishness on my own. Feeling helplessly depressed, defeated with nowhere else to turn, and with my face buried in my hands, I innocently whispered this little prayer:

> *"Jesus, if You are truly real, please come into my life and help me"*

I've highlighted this *"little backyard prayer"* for good reason, and you will soon see why. It wasn't as if I hadn't asked God to help me in the past; I had and He did. It wasn't as if I hadn't called out the name of Jesus before; I certainly had, as you know. When I'd prayed before, God would almost always help me out of the bad situation that I needed help with; but it wasn't long until I would quickly revert back to "life as normal" without any thought of God. It was like saying, "Thanks for the help; but now I'm taking control again."

This time, however, I was to find out it was going to be very different. This time something utterly implausible would slowly start happening *inside me*. In the first few days after having said that little backyard prayer, I noticed nothing unusual—nothing, that is, until a little later.

> "Unbeknownst to me, the greatest internal transformation that was to ever impact my life—and every aspect of it—had just been triggered."

What I did immediately after that little prayer was simply realize how disgusted I was with myself. I threw out the rest of the wine in my glass and simply went back into the house to face the music. Unbeknownst to me, the greatest internal transformation that was to ever impact my life—and every aspect of it—had just been triggered. I was soon going to realize that something unfathomable and life-changing had been birthed inside me.

I'll explain; and as you will clearly see, I'm talking about what started to happen with my understanding of things and with my "will" and desire to do something about this new and even revelatory knowledge. This wasn't something I was trying to work at or initiate; this is not something I had to continue to pray about. What was about to happen would happen totally on its own; it was being given to me free—and with no effort, thought or will on my part.

> "No book, person (including myself) or church was telling me what to do; it was just happening on its own."

I found myself changing into what I saw as a new, different—and what I considered a better—person. What started to happen internally was undeniable and extremely intriguing to me. I was starting to think differently, act differently, speak differently—and to want different things. No book, person (including myself) or church was telling me what to do; it was just happening on its own, and it was progressive.

Unbeknownst to me, I had just happened upon the ultimate solution in moving from torments to miracles!

I'd always considered myself a pretty good person, and a fairly successful person; but now, something had happened that was allowing me to see my real self (from the inside out) for the very first time. It was either that some unknown blinders had come off my eyes, or I had developed new internal eyes; but I was, for certain, seeing with new depth into the kind of person I really was—and I really didn't like a lot of what I saw, and wanted it changed. With these new internal eyes, I was able to examine myself from a perspective that I had never dreamt possible.

> "I didn't fight against it. Rather, I was very encouraged by it all."

My innermost mind and spirit were being given new wisdom. How could this be happening? Everything that was happening was certainly good; and everything was positive, so I didn't fight against it. Rather, I was very encouraged by it all. This change in my thinking and life was so evident to me that I actually remember stopping work in my shop one day, spellbound by how I was thinking about things, and thought quietly for a moment: "*What on earth is going on with me, anyway?*"

Born Again!

In the next few chapters, I'll describe not only some of those changes to my thinking and thought processes, but how nearly incredible circumstances started happening to help me out.

CHAPTER EIGHTEEN

Foot In Mouth

"I had one of the foulest mouths on the planet."

Thinking back, I'll be the first to admit that I had one of the foulest mouths on the planet. I actually, at one point, took pride in how many times I could curse in the course of one sentence, and still say something that I thought had some intelligence left in it. I actually thought that swearing to that extent was some type of an accomplishment—yes, sick and absurd, but that was me; and maybe even believing it was all part of being a seasoned sailor. I did, however, refrain from cursing in front of my wife and children, as well most times when other women and children were around. But because I swore with such frequency, authority and pride, I'm sure I slipped up quite often when unintended ears were around; and hence I fear I was overheard far too frequently.

I did a lot of work in my attached garage on weekends and evenings, and often customers or friends would visit me during that time. It was in my garage about a week or so after my *little backyard prayer* that my first eye-opener occurred.

I distinctly remember this happening while I was having a conversation with two male customers who came into my garage workshop that day. Only the three of us were in my workshop at the time this occurred. When I responded to one of their questions I threw in (as I often did) a couple of my so-called friendly foul adjectives (swear words) to add what I thought was emphasis to my point. I expected that they, in turn, would reciprocate by adding a couple of swear words in their responses to me. It only made sense to me that now that they knew that I was open to using foul language in my workshop, I thought they would join in by doing the same. But it didn't happen; their language was clean and professional—and for some strange reason, the fact that I had been swearing and they did not really started to bother me. I found it was uncomfortable.

Why did that bother me now? It never seemed to have bothered me before, so why now? Who were these guys, that they made me feel so convicted? Because they presented themselves professionally, authoritatively and with such clean-spoken language, I really felt I had degraded or discredited myself by using swear words in my conversation with them; and in a strange way, this now made me realize that I had devalued myself.

After they left, I thought; *"I'm really a better person than the impression I left with those two guys. How foolish I was!"* I thought to myself, *"I'm going to have to watch out from now on, that I don't make myself appear so ignorant in the future."* Never before in my life had I ever thought that my swearing was causing others to see me as ignorant. But it certainly did that time. I realized for the first time in my life that when I used curse words instead of proper English (to make myself look like I had it together), it was actually having the opposite effect on people. Hmmm. That conviction and realization was now hitting me like a ton of bricks. *Why am I degrading myself like that?* The effect that those two guys left on me was profound. I thought about how much better I'd feel about myself if I were afforded the same kind of respect from others, that I now had for them. I had never met those two men before, and I never saw them again.

> *"What started to become quite frequent...was this strange phenomenon of individuals momentarily showing up...and after them leaving, I'd realize some major impact they had made on my life."*

What started to become quite frequent over the next few months was this strange phenomenon of individuals momentarily showing up, engaging with me in some way, and after them leaving, I'd realize some major impact they had made on my life.

Allow me to digress for a moment; I'll share with you what I mean, by describing another such incident with you briefly. It wasn't long after that first occurrence that a short, very odd-looking older man walked into my shop to ingeniously help me solve a very difficult repair problem I was having with a construction laser. As it was, I saw no way to repair the laser in the time I had available; and my customer was counting on me to get this equipment repaired. The small internal part that was broken was not repairable; the laser I was working on was now outdated, and therefore had no parts available on the market that I could purchase. As a result, I was ready to give up on it, because I really thought I had no other choice. Wishing I didn't have to disappoint a good customer, I became disappointed with myself in having to give up. I breathed out what may have been a little prayer in desperation.

As I was about to start putting things away, this little odd-looking fellow knocked on my door and walked into my workshop. He was about in his sixties, and by the looks of this guy, I thought he might be looking for a handout. He casually looked around, and then asked me what I was working on. Interestingly, I decided to tell him my problem, even though I didn't think he'd understand a word about the complexity of my issue, or about construction laser equipment.

As it turned out, however, not only did he understand the problem; I could hardly believe how clever a solution he immediately gave me! What he told me, I knew, would certainly work to fix the laser. My respect and appreciation for this fellow just went through the roof, and I was embarrassed about how I had initially judged him.

Before he left my shop, he told me that my business name should not be AM Laser Repair but that I should use instead my family name, *Hnatiuk's*. He said I should be proud of my family name, and if I used it as my business name, the community would recognize that *Hnatiuk's* were willing to put their family name on the line—and therefore the business was probably worth visiting. I never forgot that wisdom, and today, all my businesses use my family name. I had never met that old man before, and I never saw him again.

"I began to realize that God was up to something new in my life."

After an ongoing number of these helpful and welcoming strangers, I began to realize that God was up to something new in my life. These strangers were momentarily showing up and engaging with me in conversation. And after they left, I would realize that they'd made some major impact on my life. These events were beginning to become commonplace.

I was quickly starting to see a pattern developing: many times, when I needed help and asked for it, God provided the solution by using people, many of whom were very kind strangers, and most of whom came into my shop to do only one thing—and that was to answer my dilemma and/or prayer; and then they left. I never saw any of them again. Sometimes I didn't immediately realize they actually were the answer to my prayer; at times it took a few minutes after they left. Then I'd slap my forehead, realizing what had just happened. In Hebrews 13:2 it states: *"Don't forget to show hospitality to strangers, for some who have done this have entertained angels without realizing it!"* I concluded that because so many of these occurrences were happening to me, this could not be happenstance.

There were many more of these angelic-type visits over the months and years that followed; but I thought it important that I mention a couple to you, so that in this way you'll better understand one of the processes God was starting to use to help me better myself and my life.

So now, let's get back to my tongue: over the next few weeks following the visit of those two very influential men, this new conviction of how ignorant I sounded hit me every time I found myself swearing. On occasion, when I'd get together with old sailor buddies, I thought I could be my old self again, forgetting about my new convictions, and knowing that my buddies would swear up a storm right alongside me. Well, yes; they did swear up a storm; but instead of me being drawn back into swearing alongside them, the strangest thing happened: when they were swearing I was hit by those similar thoughts, but now it was in defence of them: *"Wow, these great guys don't realize how their cursing is making others devalue them. I know these guys. They're good friends, intelligent and well-trained men. How can I tell them that swearing is making them look ignorant, less educated and less professional? What in the world is happening to me, anyway? I never thought like this before! Why is it bothering me so much now?"*

About four or five months after saying that *"little backyard prayer,"* I found myself standing in the middle of my workshop floor, overwhelmed by all these new and amazing little things that were happening to me. *"Something is changing inside me. It's like I'm becoming this new person inside."* Some new spirit was helping me to change from the inside out; and given what it was showing me, I wanted so much to make those changes!

"No one was telling me I shouldn't swear."

Because I didn't want to appear ignorant, and desired to feel better about myself, I started to make a concentrated effort not to swear. No one was telling me I shouldn't swear; on the contrary, it was me who desperately wanted to now get rid of that terrible habit. Having had done it for so long, it took me a good six months before I had significantly corrected my tongue.

I remember having to find ways to speak more effectively without the curse words, because up to that point I really didn't know how. I'd carefully and consciously listen to other friends and colleagues who didn't swear, to see how they expressed themselves effectively; and over time, I acquired more appropriate adjectives and a better overall command of the English language. One interesting change I made was replacing saying *"Holy Fu*k,"* with the much more fun *"Holy Smack-in, Jimmy Pappin!"*

Every now and again I'd slip up; but it happened less and less as the years went by. And now, after twenty years, it can still happen on a rare occasion. But that lesson is now behind me.

CHAPTER NINETEEN

More Clean-up

So it was with other bad habits, practices and addictions that I'd acquired over a lifetime—practices I had actually come to recognize and be comfortable with as being part of my character. Back then, I didn't have a problem with the type of person I was, and my old self would have ably defended my character and even my shortcomings. *"Sure, I have some weaknesses,"* I'd argue, *"but after all, who doesn't?"*

> *"Everything that was questionable, each in its own time, became a target for my new internal spirit."*

But amazingly, each bad habit, practice and addiction in its time started to come under my scrutiny and internal scrub board: drinking, smoking, hiding things from my wife, flirting, gambling, bending rules, credit card spending and more. This is not to say I only had bad habits; I trust I had as many good ones as bad, but everything that was questionable, each in its own time, became a target for my new internal spirit.

The most amazing part of this whole life-changing experience was that no one else was involved in telling me I should change; no one but myself, that is. No one was nagging me as to what I should or shouldn't do; instead and most astonishing, it was like there was a brand new spirit inside me, looking at things with a whole new perspective—a perspective I had never encountered before, nor thought possible. It mysteriously just started to happen, all on its own; and at times I'd often sit back and think, *"Wow! What's causing this to happen? Who is this new person inside of me?"*

> *"What new supernatural thing was happening to me now?"*

This new inner self was putting my old established character under a microscope, and saw to it that things like my impatience to situations became instead more patient and compassionate. I was starting to make more intelligent decisions; my family name and how I represented it became important; and so many other fine tunings were starting to happen. After thirty years of being forced to harbour (and suffer under) a demonic spirit, this new gentle angelic-type spirit was very welcome. *"What new supernatural thing was happening to me now?"* Whatever it was, I was certainly open to everything this one had to offer.

GO ASK THE CHIEF

Take smoking, for instance. Over my naval career, trying to quit smoking had practically become a separate career for me. I was always trying some new strategy: some gum, some program, cold turkey, weaning off, changing to menthol, doing only cigars, switching to a pipe—believe you me, whatever was out there at the time, I'd tried it! The ongoing joke on-board ship, among some of the other Chief Petty Officers, was when young sailors were trying to quit smoking the Chiefs would tell them to go and ask Chief Hnatiuk how to quit. "Yes, go and ask Chief Hnatiuk how to quit—because he has quit more times than anyone else we know," they'd jokingly tease.

With cigarettes so cheap in the navy, I jokingly told people that I couldn't afford to quit smoking—or drinking, for that matter. In 1970, at the ship's canteen, I paid ten cents for a large pack of cigarettes, and I was allowed two packs a day. "Hey, I enjoy smoking, so why should I bother to quit?" I'd quickly tell others who may have suggested I quit. But then, after close to thirty years of smoking, my body was certainly telling me otherwise.

*"A couple of months after that **little** backyard prayer..."*

A couple of months after that *"little backyard prayer,"* an uncanny process started to happen inside me; and each factor of that process gradually started to change my thinking. In bed, hearing my wheezing when breathing started to bother me—hmmm, it never bothered me before. When I brushed my teeth, the yellow left on my front teeth looked unattractive—hmmm, that never bothered me before. I could actually smell the yellow on my fingers; again, hmmm. I started to see how some people were politely annoyed by cigarette smoke and cigarettes butts. Hmmm, why was it that all these things that hadn't bothered me in the past, all of a sudden became front and centre in my thinking?

No one was telling me or suggesting to me that I should stop smoking. But I was increasingly becoming very aware of and very self-educated in the whole concept of smoking, and all its negative effects. Why now? Why hadn't this happened before? I'd been trying to quit, on-again, off-again for over twenty years; but now the evidence of the need to quit for my own good was piling sky-high in my mind, and nobody was forcing anything on me; it was all coming from inside me—and I found this *very* interesting.

There was, however, one critical factor and major obstacle that wouldn't change. That was the difference between ending my swearing habit and now wanting to end my smoking habit.

Swearing had to do with overcoming a mental habit; but smoking was a powerful physical addiction as well. Big difference. So, recognizing my past repeated failures at quitting smoking, I found myself saying, *"Sorry God; even though I want to quit, I don't have the strength, or the way, or the will-power to see this one through."*

> *"God most often doesn't just wave a magic wand to fix your problems."*

Once again, watch what you pray for! Over these years, I've come to realize all too well that God most often doesn't just wave a magic wand to fix your problems; hardly ever, in fact. Most times there's some hardship you have to endure in the middle of the process. The greater the potential reward, the greater the pain to get it; but I've found that the reward is always much greater than the pain; and on completion of each answered prayer, I'd always wish I had initiated the process earlier, irrespective the consequences in between.

Quitting smoking ended up being a major physical painful experience for me. In the past, all my attempts to quit smoking were defeated by my addiction; but this time, God saw to it that the challenge would have nothing to do with the addiction factor; it would, however, have everything to do with my physical health. In other words, I got so sick physically that smoking wasn't even on my mind.

In 1993, two years before retiring from the navy, I came down with double pneumonia. Both my lungs were inflamed by a bacterial or viral infection; their air sacs filled with pus that became solid. That was coupled with an additional infectious and nauseating malady that had me flat on my back for days. I was not only believing I might die—and at times wishing I would die, to escape the pain—but the thought of smoking during this experience never even crossed my mind; I was far too sick, and my lungs were burning, to the point that it was difficult for me to breathe at all.

After the three to four weeks it took me to fully recover, the diminished urge to start smoking was easily defeated by the thoughts of the pain from which I had just recovered. Also on my mind were all those new convictions that had started to annoy me about my smoking, just before I got sick. I was finally able to kick the addiction—and as you can see, it wasn't without pain; but well worth it, regardless. It's been twenty-two years now that I haven't smoked a cigarette or anything else. I was also happy to read in medical research reports that twenty years after quitting smoking, a person's lungs have been restored to what they would have been if they had never smoked. Another mission accomplished!

DRINKING SOLUTION

I'll admit that I had every symptom of being a part-time alcoholic. I could probably go a couple of weeks without a drink; but all too often, once I started drinking I didn't know when to quit—or rather, I was having far too much "fun" to quit. What held me back from more frequent abuse of alcohol was that I held down an important and responsible job, and I often had to perform at my maximum potential in order to get the job done. My responsibility to my family and career weighed heavily on me, as it should have. So I was very mindful of hangovers or missing work as a result of drinking, and those two factors often curbed my desire to pass the point of no return when having a couple of ales.

I would guess that I was pretty much a "happy drunk," and I was forever the party organizer so that I didn't have to drink alone. As I explained earlier, what came to disgust me most was the increasingly horrible hangovers the "mornings after," which in time became responsible for initiating that innocent but powerful little prayer in the backyard.

> "I prayed that He would show me instead how to once again drink responsibly and in moderation."

My prayers, after that backyard incident having to do with my alcohol abuse, were not so much asking God to have me "quit drinking" completely; surely, I believed, I didn't have to quit drinking altogether, as so many of my friends had to do! Rather, my prayer was asking God to please "restore me." I prayed that He would show me instead how to once again drink responsibly and in moderation, as so many others are able to do. I heard many great things about Alcoholics Anonymous (AA), but I saw total sobriety more as a punishment; and I wanted something better than that. My God, my personal Friend, a most powerful God with intelligence beyond measure, surely could afford me a better solution then having to quit completely! That's what I asked of God, and I was convinced He could help me to do just that. True to God's form, the internal changes then started.

It was over a period of about a year that my desire to attend drinking parties simply diminished to a point of becoming nonexistent. An activity that I had regularly encouraged, I was now avoiding and making excuses not to attend. It wasn't something I had to force myself to do; on the contrary, I simply and amazingly lost the desire to go. This change in my desire and attitude was also so obvious, so different for me, that I again had to sit back at times and take notice of what was happening: *"Wow! How was it that I'd lost the desire to go to drinking parties?"* I accepted this change; but I still found the process inside me intriguing.

Over that same year, when, what, and how much I could drink became increasingly clear to me. Beer, even one bottle—even a half bottle—started giving me incredible headaches, minutes after starting to drink—a complete one hundred and eighty degree shift, because in the past a beer would help me get rid of a headache. A beer had also tasted so good after some tiring work on a very hot day; but now it started causing me to have a headache within minutes. If I didn't stop, the headache increased in intensity with every swallow. This became an obvious red flag and warning that beer would not be on God's menu of alcoholic beverages I was going to enjoy going forward. I've accepted that fact.

I had only one recurrence of what I called over-drinking since that *"little backyard prayer"*; and that was a few years later at my daughter's wedding. My enchantment at this special event had me foolishly throw caution to the wind—oops! I'm not perfect, and I still make mistakes. I promptly apologized for it, and ever since then I've "put a cap on it." That was more than fifteen years ago.

So now, after twenty years, am I happy with the outcome of my request to God? I absolutely am! I didn't have to stop drinking altogether, but my former desire to drink as I did, to the point of intoxication, completely vanished. My drinking is pretty well limited to having a glass of choice wine, such as Chardonnay, with Ellen with our meal, or when casually relaxing with family and friends. Any desire to drink beyond that just doesn't exist.

So it was with each of the other convictions on my bad behaviour list: each, in its own time, amazingly came under my own personal scrutiny. Each has its own story how God enabled me to deal with it; each unique, challenging—yet most rewarding.

Now, after twenty years, would I say that the process is complete? Certainly not! Nor will it ever be while on this planet. I will say that God took care, first and foremost, of those character traits that were the most offensive; and now that those have been dealt with, God has me dealing with other interesting, challenging and life-changing initiatives.

FIGURING OUT WHAT HAD HAPPENED

*"Let's get back to that so-called **little backyard prayer** I keep referring to."*

So for a couple of minutes, let's get back to that so-called *little backyard prayer* I keep referring to. After all, when I prayed that prayer, I was hung over, drinking before breakfast on a Sunday, and cursing my blackout from the evening before. So, it's not like I deserved to have God come alongside to help me out. What happened that time that was so different from all the other times I had prayed? Because I could definitely see that everything that started to happen—all those internal changes—definitely stemmed back to having said that *little prayer.*

Each time I'd sit back and question God about what was happening to me, He reminded me of that *little prayer.*

I remember how ridiculous I thought the explanation was, that a few Christians had given me years earlier, about something like this being possible. They had told me that the Holy Spirit of God, if honestly invited, would in fact become resident inside a person. They explained that God is a gentleman, and doesn't push himself on anyone. They had explained that the Bible points out that you have to actually invite God into your life; and if anyone honestly and wholeheartedly does, the Holy Spirit will actually come in and become resident inside you; but He will *not*, if you don't specifically *ask*. When I said that little backyard prayer, I had first admittedly told God that I was sorry for being such an idiot, and that I truly wanted Him to come into my life and help me. Prior to this, all my prayers to God were simply asking Him to take care of specific problems I was experiencing. In contrast, the *little backyard prayer* actually invited Him to come in and take over my life. Big difference!

"The more I thought about it, things were starting to make a whole lot more sense."

At the time they were explaining these things to me, I found such an explanation pretty hypothetical and without much substance, especially when I looked around at some of those who claimed to have invited the Holy Spirit to come into their lives. However, now—and with what I was experiencing—I certainly felt that maybe, just maybe, what they'd told me had some truth. I was starting to put all these ducks in a row; and the more I thought about it, things were starting to make a whole lot more sense. After all, I was certainly experiencing a new and welcome, truly wonderful spirit inside me.

Then that crazy term I'd heard over the years, "born again," started to come into play. The term was really meaningless to me, because first and foremost, it simply didn't make any sense. As I saw it then, having to become a "born again" person looked like far too much work; and with a whole lot of rules I'd never be able to keep, nor enjoy doing.

But now, I had every reason to believe that this "born again" thing could in fact be what was happening to me, inside. It was also the only thing that offered any kind of explanation about my internal change. All of this was truly and absolutely amazing; these new internal eyes, these helpful convictions, my new thought processes, my new and improved attitudes had me becoming like a new person; it *was* sort of like being born again! What was happening was indeed supernatural, and certainly miraculous. What the Bible says in Romans 12:2 was starting to make some sense: *"Do not be conformed to this world, but be transformed by the renewal of your mind..."* My mind was truly undergoing an astonishing transformation—all by itself.

CHAPTER TWENTY

Out of Hiding

"That evil thing was simply waiting for its most opportune time to strike again."

If you recall, some chapters ago I shared with you a victory I had over a powerful demonic voice that tormented me in my truck as I drove home from work. Every time that voice would open its mouth, I threatened it by telling it I would pray the Lord's Prayer out loud. I was relentless in keeping my promise, and eventually I won that battle; the voice went quiet and appeared to have departed for good. Yes, it *appeared* to have gone away, but in fact—and most disappointing—was what I didn't realize: it only went into hiding, or went dormant. I came to understand that it had been able to simply go into hiding because *I hadn't dealt with it properly at the time*, and now that evil thing was simply waiting for its most opportune time to strike again. And it most certainly did—with a vengeance, eight years later. Imagine that: it waited *eight years*!

Aside from the normal trials and tribulations of everyday life that were part and parcel of learning through experience, all outright demonic attacks had ceased since that *little backyard prayer* established my new on-going relationship with God. I was eight years free from demonic torments of any form! Yes, life and God were challenging me to grow spiritually; but I was very pleased with the progress in my amazing transformation, and I found my new freedom in life indescribably welcome. As to where this demonic thing had been residing over the past eight years, I'm unsure. But as hell would have it, the time the demonic *thing* decided to re-enter my life was when I was experiencing one of the most exciting and most wonderful times I could imagine. Thinking back, I don't know of a more opportune time that ugly *thing* could have surfaced to spoil my happiness than when it did. Instead of having me experience one of those horrific out-of-body torments that I'd suffered from for more than thirty years, this time it was attempting to have me experience the same horror in real life! It knew the exact hour, as if an alarm clock had gone off. That *thing* had been patiently waiting eight years for my first grandson to be born.

"All my grandchildren have a very special place in their grandfather's heart."

I could never have imagined the joy I would feel when my first grandson was born; it was like seventh heaven, and certainly a memorable pinnacle in my life. I was grinning from ear to ear. All my grandchildren have a very special place in their grandfather's heart. They're a marvellous generation, and a joy to have around; and that first experience was like discovering a new incredible world of joy.

But as only hell could have devised, the snake started to cleverly infiltrate my mind with a vengeance. It appeared to be the same demon that I had humiliated and forced to be quiet eight years earlier; and it was as though it had now decided to get even.

It happened a few weeks after my first grandson was born. The boy was an absolute joy to our household, and everyone longed to be able to hold and cuddle the little fella. I treasured those times, and especially when it was my turn to hold him; my joy was overwhelming. The baby was an absolute treasure. I could never have believed that anything could at this point spoil my joy; but after a few weeks, something unimaginably and devastatingly did. A demon started to infiltrate my thinking. *"My God,"* I thought, *"where in hell did that thought come from? Why now, of all times?"*

> *"I was able to recognize almost immediately that I had an unwanted visitor."*

After having to deal for so many years with demonic forces fighting for my mind, I was able to recognize almost immediately that I had an unwanted visitor; and I was shocked.

I considered myself a friend of the most-high God, and I believed that devils had no right to be in me or around me any more. I believed I had been faithful in my walk with God to the core now for years. So what on earth was going on? From what could only have been from the depths of hell, a whisper started to tamper with the thought processes within my mind. It had me believe that I shouldn't hold the child, because I was not mentally stable. I couldn't believe what I was thinking! It started having me believe that my mind was going to break, just as my father's had when I was six years old; and I would totally lose control of what I was doing. That *thing* in my mind gave me no peace; the thought infiltrations were continuous, and allowed me absolutely no quiet time with my grandson. I was sickened by fear of what I might do if I were to lose control of my mind; could that actually happen? My mind was causing me to believe that I'd have to commit suicide after coming to my senses, and realizing what I had done to my grandson and others in my family while I was under its control.

I couldn't believe this was happening! I was absolutely devastated, and my heart virtually collapsed. From that point, every time I was handed the child to hold, that ugly *thing* would immediately start its rhetoric. The thoughts it forced into my mind were so convincing that tears poured from my eyes. I'd quickly turn away and wipe my face, so that no one would see what was happening; and then I'd turn and immediately ask my daughter or my wife to take the child from me. I'd make an excuse that I had to go and do something, and would exit the room—and often the house. Heartbroken, I cried out to God to help me. I couldn't believe how I was being robbed of one of the greatest joys in life, that I had just come to experience. How could I ever again enjoy my family? *"Why me, God? What did I do to deserve this?"*

I became desperate to find a solution, and knew that I had to force myself to start thinking about this logically. I'd had to deal with these powerful deceptive spirits before, and I wasn't going to go down without a fight this time, either. Analyzing the patterns of these mental manipulations had convinced me that this was not being generated by me, but rather that I was again under a demonic assault. Once I understood that the despicable *thing* was back, my prayers for help were properly directed.

God put it on my heart to speak to two pastors whom I knew fairly well. They happened to be a husband-and-wife team, and they pastored a little Pentecostal church within walking distance from our home. I didn't attend this church regularly, but on occasion my wife and I would attend special events that they held. These pastors were very approachable, very friendly and convincingly dedicated to the power of God and prayer. We loved visiting them. As God would have it, I found myself dropping in, unannounced, to their little office downstairs; and they immediately gave me some private time. I trusted them enough to tell them everything about this demonic mental manipulation, and they certainly saw that I was sick about this new development. They saw that my heart was broken, and that I desperately needed help. I was very specific in what I told them, because I didn't want anything or any unknown information to stand in the way of them determining how this had to be dealt with.

> *"I understood now that I was inflicted with a 'generational curse."*

After some preliminary discussion, they both agreed and explained to me that I needed *"deliverance"* from the *"spirit of death."* They helped me understand that it was most likely as a result of the trauma that I had experienced as a child. The demon (*the spirit of death*) that had possessed my father had a window of opportunity during my childhood trauma to become resident in me. It was now manifesting at its most opportune times during my life, to see if it could have me cause harm to my family, as it did with my father. It had failed in its attempts to have me harm my wife eight years earlier, so now it was trying a new deceptive manipulation. I understood now that I was inflicted with a *"generational curse,"* and I needed to be delivered from it. Just as important, I had to also ensure that this curse would be broken—stopped forever—and that it could never be passed down to my children and/or their children. The Bible mentions "generational curses" in several places: Exodus 20:5, Numbers 14:18 and Deuteronomy 5:9.

I was helped to understand that even though I had accepted Christ into my life, the curses that had already been passed down to me before I came into covenant with God still had some rights over me. However, because I had accepted Christ into my life and was now being transformed by the renewing of my mind, I had the legal grounds to be cleared and free from the curses. Because of Christ's crucifixion and my alliance with Him, I was told the curses could be broken. *"Therefore, if anyone is in Christ, he is a new creation. The old has passed away; behold, the new has come."* (2 Corinthians 5:17) So the only thing left to do was to cast out any spirits that had gained entrance, or rights to afflict me, before I had accepted Christ. The two pastors agreed to set up a special meeting with me to have "deliverance." I agreed to their solution. I was very thankful, and the meeting was planned. I went home with a renewed sense of hope, and could hardly wait for the meeting.

The following week I showed up, as planned, to their little office at their church; and I could certainly see the importance they put into the process that they had planned for the evening. Once we started, they prayed for protection, and then they called upon numerous scriptures having to do with the power of Christ to deal with the *"spirit of death"* and any other lingering evil spirits that were influencing my mind, body and soul. Their knowledge of Scripture was remarkable, and I could understand why God had me land on their doorstep. *"Thank you, Father in heaven!"* After considerable prayer, they spoke directly to the demon that was manipulating my mind; they spoke to it as if I wasn't even in the room; they had the demon bound in Jesus' name and confidently commanded the *"spirit of death"* and all its cohorts to leave me, in the name of Jesus Christ of Nazareth. This very intense process took about fifteen minutes, and they then prayed for the protection of my whole family, and that the curse be broken.

Prior to departing, they explained some of the things that I could expect in the next few days, and possibly for even a few weeks. They told me that the demon would most likely hang around long enough to tell me that the *deliverance* didn't work, and he'd probably be fairly persistent with this lie. They explained how I was to have some dedicated prayer time every day, and how to ensure my home was worthy to have the Lord reside in it. I thanked them very much for their help, and proceeded to walk home.

> *"I told it to go to hell, because in time that's where it was to end up, anyway."*

Well, as sure as God made little green apples, I wasn't five minutes down the road when a distant whisper started telling me that what I had just done had been a complete waste of everyone's time. I immediately chuckled and thought, *"Wow! That didn't take long!"* True to what the pastors had told me, I could see that the liar was doing just what we expected it would. I told the demon that it was a defeated foe, and that the blood of Jesus Christ had given me the right to have it removed from my life forever. I told it to go to hell, because in time that's where it was to end up, anyway. Just as important, I remembered to dedicate time each evening to prayer, and to see that anything that would displease God was removed from my household. That included monitoring books, CDs, objects, pictures and even what TV programs we watched, to ensure that nothing displeasing to God remained in or entered our house.

I knew that the true test would come when I got to hold my grandson again; and after a few days, I decided to make that happen. I can tell you now that I couldn't have been a happier grandpa! I was finally able to cuddle the little fella and not be distracted by that infidel. Truly, it was a momentous victory, having that vile *"thing"* dealt with and gone from my life!

I was also very excited to let those two pastors know the outcome of their efforts.

In no time, I realized that my family life was amazingly back on track. It was truly like a homecoming; and no one but me was the wiser as to what had happened. It was a greater homecoming than what I had experienced on arriving home from sea, even after a six month NATO deployment. My life had been virtually restored! It was amazing!

It's been over fourteen years now, and I've had the distinct pleasure of having three additional wonderful grandsons added to our family—with the promise of more. Once again the Bible was true to its word, and I have effectively closed the book on that generational curse. My family and I are henceforth protected. *"Christ redeemed us from the curse"* (Galatians 3:13); and *"If [Christ] sets you free, you will be free indeed"* (John 8:36).

CHAPTER TWENTY-ONE

Spin-offs

As a result of being taken in the spirit and being allowed to come alongside God, I also felt that He was telling me, *"Now that you have had the privilege of witnessing My love and power first-hand, know that I am with you always as you go forward."* At that, I also started to have thoughts that God may be preparing me to do something that I was yet unaware of—something that might require extraordinary faith. Was He showing me such powerful things because He knew I'd need a solid foundation to endure what was to come? Or was it solely because I had requested that I see Him, as a result of purifying my heart?

"I now had a profound appreciation of how real, and powerful, enormous and approachable God was."

Regardless the reason, I knew that in the interim, I'd be able to harness and exercise this new knowledge of God in a meaningful way. One thing was certain: after those powerful experiences, whenever my life was undergoing trials, and regardless of how severe the trial, I now had a profound appreciation of how real, and powerful, enormous and approachable God was—which lessened any burden I was experiencing. I found that even amidst the greatest of difficulties, if I could divorce myself long enough from my problem, I now had a place of refuge to which I could go. There I could find marvellous peace, a peace like no other. But I still had to remember to seek that place of refuge, which is often not the first place people habitually seek as a solution when confronted with adversity.

I found that I now had the assurance that God was so much bigger, so much more relevant than anything else that happened around me; that He is ultimately in control of everything; and that everything has a purpose, regardless of how ungodly that "everything" may seem. It's a totally different mindset than what I'd previously had. My mind could now go to that place, and be comforted by the fact of how small my problems were in comparison to the big picture. This was wonderfully comforting, especially when confronted with major adversities.

CHAPTER TWENTY-TWO

Relevance

"Many others can find solutions to what they now think are impossible problems.

Another question I hope you're asking is about yourself and/or a friend or family member, and what relevance all this information might have in *your* lives. Is there someone else who might be able to benefit from this information? Can there be any relevance in what I'm sharing and what I'm about to share, that may be beneficial to you or a loved one? Because of what I've lived through and learned, I'm certain that others—many others—can find solutions to what they now think are impossible problems.

Others will read this and know that they can start to identify deception and demonic bondage, and eventually experience freedom from it; and also, to go so far as to transition into a life with miracles even greater than what I enjoy and treasure. Please understand that transitioning into a life that has miracles and a relationship with God doesn't require a previous life similar to mine. Absolutely not! Be assured, *anyone* can enjoy a personal relationship with God the same as I have—and more; but it still does require a most important transition from whatever your current state is, to one that I'm about to explain to you. Before I explain that transition, let's look at relevance.

I can say, with every assurance, that if someone you know actually admits to hearing voices, there is every possibility that he or she isn't making it up. If someone says they are being tormented by demons, there is every possibility that the demon is as real as the problem they're describing. It shouldn't be assumed that the voices or the demons are a fabrication of that person's mind; otherwise the treatment will solely deal with the person's mind, when the actual problem is the demon—who has no business being there. Let me assure you again, demonic voices are real and demons are real; and if that fact isn't recognized as true, and treated as such, the recipient (the patient) will most likely remain a patient indefinitely. Prescription drugs may comfort and incapacitate the patient by numbing and dumbing down his or her brain (and thus the mind); but be assured, the attacker remains undisturbed, unharmed—and is most assuredly accomplishing its mission. You should consider: why is it that the demonic has opted to attack and incapacitate you and/or your friend or loved one? What potential threat are they to the demonic world? What great thing are you and/or they being held back from achieving?

"Remember, demonic deception usually begins as something inviting and attractive, even appearing normal and good."

In an earlier chapter, I alluded that everyone is a potential target for this enemy of the mind. Everyone. Christian evangelist and author Joyce Myers writes specifically about this in her book *The Battlefield of the Mind*. Remember, demonic deception usually begins as something inviting and attractive, even appearing normal and good; but in the end, if you succumb to it (and you will), the deception will lead to at least irrelevance and a waste of your time, and most probably some hardship and pain down the road. That is his intent—and those are the mild cases. Ultimately, he intends to steal, kill and destroy.

The full cycle of the deception could take anywhere from a day to years to complete; and the devil doesn't care, as long as he eventually gets his twisted job done. To believe that you are not a target for this enemy, or not under his influence in some way, either you require further study on the matter, or you have already been won over by the deception. Remember, the enemy has no desire to show you his evil side unless it's absolutely necessary; he easily wins most people over by appearing as the *angel of light*. I can only recommend that you be mindful of this, and be willing to investigate your situations and your life with this knowledge in mind.

Then there are the extreme cases. Many struggling people, who experience symptoms similar to mine, or other supernatural demonic encounters, could be diagnosed as having schizophrenia, being bipolar, or some other similar mental disorders. Regardless of what the professionals and/or society wish to label it, if the treatment fails to take into consideration the possibility of the supernatural being real, and that the problem exists within that supernatural, then the treatment can miss the mark completely. It certainly would have missed the mark in my case.

> *"The same could or can be happening to your friends or family members."*

I have to believe that there are countless individuals, including some in mental intuitions, who have been diagnosed thus, and hence are heavily sedated with powerful medications that make them virtual zombies. If this had been done to me, I would have ended up being imprisoned by powerful medications, with little chance of explaining my situation coherently or being believed. The result would have been being trapped, and having to live with the demons indefinitely. The same could or can be happening to your friends or family members. Consider this: where else does a person end up, when they tell people that demons are screaming at them to kill someone? Yes, it's important that they be taken seriously; but equally important that whoever will be responsible for their treatment be equally open to what the Scriptures recommend about such situations.

In my case, I had enough sense to realize something was amiss; and I took the time to analyze my own situation. I also had the distinct advantage of having had to cope with many years of demonic torment, to fully realize that I was most certainly dealing with nothing other than the supernatural. Because of the earlier torments, I *knew* without a doubt that the supernatural was very real; so by the time the voices actually started, I was already on to their trickery.

If you recall, once I told the voice (the demon) that was screaming at me that I knew who he was, the demon stopped the deception of trying to pretend he was part of my mind, and he gave up trying to make me think I was going insane. At that point, he openly revealed himself as a separate creature—the demonic spirit it was.

For the most part, I never doubted my sanity; and therefore I had the sense to keep quiet about my torments, and later about the voices. I was able to function normally and successfully ninety-five percent of the time, and it was only the suddenness of the attacks five percent of the time that had me in shackles, and at war with that creature within myself. The difference between who I was most of the time, and what was attacking me periodically, was so different that I *knew* the attacker was not inherently part of my mind, my spirit or my person. Therefore, knowing that it wasn't of me, and that these things were supernatural, my challenge was trying to figure it out; and until I did, I needed to find ways to keep the devils at bay—and I did. Under those conditions,

I secretly watched how the demonic activity operated within me. I was watching their every move, without allowing the demon(s) to know that I was keeping track. To do this, I had to differentiate between which of my thoughts were genuine and which were possibly deceptions; not an easy task—in fact, very difficult—but after thirty years of practice, I had become pretty good at it. You may recall how I had to trick myself into a meeting with Gord's mom, and how I tested my spirit-walks; that's an example of the convoluted type of thinking I had to have, knowing that there was a devil within.

"There are many levels of deception, from the very mild to the very severe."

Many of you may have friends and/or family about whom you are perplexed or disappointed, thinking that they're going off the deep end. There are many levels of deception, from the very mild to the very severe. My own I would assess as having experienced the full spectrum, including the extreme. In a lot of cases, professionals will suggest that the underlying cause of such conditions is a traumatic event earlier in life; and in most cases, I believe that to be a correct analysis. It certainly was in my case. Where the medical profession is failing, in many cases, is what the treatment should be. I didn't go to professionals, because I suspected—with good reason—that they'd treat me as "mentally disturbed," and prescribe powerful medications; and my career, marriage and even my life, as I knew it, would have ended. By today, I fear, I'd have become a sixty-five-year-old zombie, pacing the floor of a mental institution, trapped by powerful medications keeping me incapacitated—and nobody being the wiser. But because I was able to diagnose the symptoms as supernatural, my adversary was correctly identified and eventually effectively dealt with. This resulted in being able to live a very successful life, and one that can now expose the powerful deceptions of that enemy—an action he was desperately trying to prevent me from doing.

What I didn't know then, that I know today, is that I was under what the Bible refers to as a *generational curse*; and I believe the same type of demon to which my biological father had become a victim was bombarding me. So yes; I definitely needed help. But at that point, I didn't trust either the medical profession or the church. That, in part, is what I was dealing with, and the predicament that I was in.

I certainly believe that in some cases, there are brains and/or minds that malfunction as a result of physical injury or psychological trauma, and these may not be influenced in any way whatsoever by demonic activity. Those are most obviously out of the realm of

"It's unfortunate that a partnership of sorts...isn't available between the medical profession and the liturgical profession."

my expertise, and in such cases, we have to appreciate and rely on the learned medical and mental professional institutions. It's unfortunate that a partnership of sorts—a working relationship—isn't available between the medical profession and the liturgical profession, when dealing with such important problems as these. This lack of liaison is the result of professional minds that are blinded just as mine was, and therefore unable to see the truth because they have yet to believe. Until they do, they will not, because they cannot, recognize that our lives are affected by both the natural and the supernatural.

In this book, I'm speaking specifically to a condition that obviously requires supernatural treatment, and possibly even physical restraint, until the necessary supernatural therapy alleviates the attacker. Most, if not all, medical professionals are sadly disallowed to even mention, in the course of their diagnosis and therapy, that demonic activity may be what has to be dealt with. Here I'm speaking specifically to cases of those who complain or show signs of abnormal mental activity connected to something traumatic in their past—their youth, in many cases. In those cases, I truly believe there is a good likelihood that their brain may be as normal as mine. There are about thirty-five scriptures that warn us that Satan is not only good at deception, but that he is in fact the master of deception. What chance do you think you, alone, have against such a master deceiver? Do you think you are the sole exception? I beg to differ! The Bible states categorically in Revelation 12:9, *"Satan, who deceives the whole world."* So there are no exceptions, and only one solution to Satan's deception; and I thank God that I found it!

I truly believe that it's not just me, but many are dealing one-on-one with the demonic world just as I was; and I hope that most are dealing with it to a lesser degree than I was. But remember, regardless of how many ways I tried to free myself, it wasn't until I truly found the *key* that true freedom came. One would have to wonder, after so many years of me crying out to God for help, why that help didn't come. What was the *key*? Why did help finally come, and how did I make that transition?

CHAPTER TWENTY-THREE

Know This

> *"What I've shared with you encapsulates an aspect of the supernatural that is rarely spoken about."*

What I've shared with you encapsulates an aspect of the supernatural that is rarely spoken about, or ever experienced by most. I've taken care to describe my experiences accurately and to the best of my ability. In all honesty, I can assure you that what I have painstakingly shared with you is true in every detail. Aside from my word, I have only my reputation, my accomplishments and those who will vouch for my character to offer you as reassurance that, even though these pages may have suggested otherwise, these writings come from a person who is known to be stable and reliable. Most reassuring and ultimately rewarding is that you don't have to take my word for it; you, yourself, can put all this to the test.

> *"So don't be discouraged, but rather be encouraged."*

What I really want my readers to understand is how you can benefit from what I've discovered in all this. What a waste of my life, and what a shame it would be for me to die and take this to the grave without telling others! What I've discovered is truly a way to unlock the door to some of the most bewildering mysteries of life; doors that are meant to be open, but because of deception are sadly not even visible to most good, everyday people. This life, for me, has been a long, often frightening battle; but my rewards and victories vastly diminish the anguish and hardships of that journey. So don't be discouraged, but rather be encouraged.

I'm reminded of when I was on a total immersion French course in Saint Jean, Quebec in the mid-1980s. One of the activities that I found a lot of fun, even though challenging, was a "Road Rally Scavenger Hunt," conducted entirely in French. There were three English-speaking students per vehicle; the two who weren't driving would work together and try to decipher the written clues (all in French), and so provide directions to the driver. We had a lot of laughs, even though at times we made mistakes and got off course. It was a way to discover the community and the culture we were in, and a way to learn the terminology of the French language. At the end of the day, there were prizes for the winners, and a celebration barbecue.

"Do you recall my challenge to God in Chapter 13 of this book?

If you recall, earlier in this book it was only because of a defiant challenge that I had given God, and then because of His subsequent response, that I came to realize that the most incredible and exciting "scavenger hunt" was actually contained within the pages of the Bible. Do you recall my challenge to God in Chapter 13 of this book? I wrote:

My nature was that of a skeptic; and because of the claims of the Bible, I felt that what the Bible stated should be expected to stand at face value. In other words, if the Bible dared to make bold statements and claimed to be true, then I felt that I had the right to be equally bold and challenge God to own up to that what is written in the Bible.

I'll be quoting some of the statements in the Bible with which I had real issues, so it's important that I show you where in the Bible I found those statements. You should know that each major segment of the Bible is called a "book," and each book has a name; then each chapter in that book has a number; and each verse in each chapter has a number. So I can easily identify the places where you can find my references, just in case you happen to have a Bible and want to check out what I'm claiming.

It is in 2 Timothy 3:16, it says that God inspired the different authors of the Bible to write what they did. When I read that, I figured, "That's just great; if God told them what to write then everything in the Bible must be true, right?" OK; that's when I figured I'd soon be checking out to see if that was true.

A goal of mine was also to find out if someone could actually get closer to God. Was that just a myth, or simply an inner sense or feeling that some people claim to have had? Was it really just emotionalism? Also, is that literally what the Bible was stating or talking about? Just how close can you get to God if you are still alive and in this world?

As you might expect, I was very pleased to find in the Bible where it states: "Draw near to God, and he will draw near to you" (James 4:8). "Really!" I thought. "Well that's just great, isn't it? If God had the author write that, it must be true, right? So let's see if that's possible."

> *"It was my skepticism of what was written in the Bible that had me challenge it."*

So it started out. It was my skepticism of what was written in the Bible that had me challenge it; and only then was I eventually able to find out the astonishing truth it contained. I'll remind you that it took persistence; but I could never have imagined it would reveal so much to someone as undeserving and ungodly as me. At the time, I was a bit of a heretic, to say the least. In my early years, the Bible was no more than a glorified storybook about things that may have happened in the past. Yes, a few years later—but before my actual encounters with God—I got where I respected the Bible to a point; but I certainly didn't take it literally as truth. I may have told you I did, more because I didn't want to upset God (just in case He existed); but deep down, I didn't actually live my life utilizing the knowledge the Bible provides. Hosea 4:6 states, *"My people are destroyed from lack of knowledge. Because you have rejected knowledge, I also will reject you."* And true to His word, it was only when I became infatuated with wanting to know everything I could about God, did He finally reveal Himself to me and stop rejecting me.

"I work hard, so I'm allowed to play hard."

Why on earth did God have time for me? At the time of my encounter with Him, my mind was often *a* cesspool; and my character, in a lot of ways, was very offensive. My mind was blinded to just how offensive I was, and I would actually defend and justify my bad behaviour as being something I'd "earned the right" to have. *"I work hard, so I'm allowed to play hard,"* I'd sadly claim. So, yes; I came to realize that I was certainly an undeserving candidate for God to come alongside; but it was reassuring to find out that the Bible is full of history that illustrates how God uses imperfect people. Moses started out a murderer, but later became the humblest man in the world; and we know how God used him! The Apostle Paul put followers of Jesus to death; but God abruptly changed him into the greatest witness to the Gentiles for Christ. Hot-headed Peter, originally named Simon—the one who denied Jesus repeatedly—was an apostle ordained by Jesus; and he became a leader of God's Church on earth. So, I'm thankful that I have a God who uses imperfect people and is so forgiving.

"I wish I'd understood the process before I started."

That being realized, I can say with confidence that there is hope for everyone, regardless of what you've done or what you're doing. No one has to clean up his or her act before asking God for help. On the contrary, and as I came to experience, it's only once you sincerely ask for help that God comes in to provide that help; and then He (not you) ends up doing the cleaning up for you. That's what I found so amazing! I was able to continue to do only what I wanted to do; but God saw that I was given the Holy Spirit, who renewed my mind to do it—and to change what I wanted to do. I wish I'd understood the process before I started; it would have made things a whole lot easier for me. All that said, I see this as now giving you a wonderful advantage, should you decide to use this information appropriately.

Another thing to start watching for are what I refer to as "mini-miracles." Once the untold number of mini-miracles started to happen to me, I soon came to realize that these were not at all coincidences, but rather, they were all "God-incidences." Intrigued by them, I then started to keep a journal (a record) of the most significant ones. Once you initiate your own journey, I recommend that you start consciously recognizing the pattern of how things are being solved in your life. Had you asked for help? Did it come out perfect? Make a record of it.

"Having God actually participate in your 'scavenger hunt' is anything but boring!"

It was later, through study and digging through the many translations of the Bible—and talking to God like I was talking to a friend, even getting angry with God as I would with a friend—and consulting with clergy and many friends, that the whole process became like an exciting "scavenger hunt." As I've shared with you, having God actually participate in your "scavenger hunt" is anything but boring! In fact, He fills the journey with unimaginable wonder! Approaching the Bible from this perspective is nothing less than an indescribable adventure. Be persistent; it's only as difficult as you make it.

My journey was triggered by torments, as a result of how I was impacted by a childhood trauma; your journey will obviously be different—but nevertheless, just as important as mine. I'm convinced that regardless of where you currently are in your belief about God, it can become exceedingly and amazingly better. Whether you're an atheist, a mocker of religion, a modest believer, or even a lifelong avid and dedicated believer in Christ, what God has done and continues to do for me, He will also do for you—and more. You only have to take Him at His word; believe me when I say, that's what He wants you to do! Life was not meant to be mundane, but rather filled with purpose—His purpose.

> *"A key is keeping your focus on pursuing God, not on your problem."*

In sharing my story with you and the world, my plan is to give you every key I possess, and every means I currently know that has led to my successful relationship with the Creator of the universe—and all the rewards that entails and will entail. You have to know that regardless the obstacles that stand in your way today, regardless of how insurmountable they seem, there is hope to overcome them. Your miracle is possible; you simply need to seek God with *a* passion. A key is keeping your focus on pursuing God, not on your problem. The unfathomable and unimaginably powerful and loving God that I met is waiting to do that with you.

Whether your problem is as simple as being frustrated by not having a paper-clip, or to the point that life is so difficult that you may be considering suicide, God wants to be involved in helping you; and He *will* help you in the most astonishing ways.

By the way: don't tell God how to fix your problem! Let Him decide that. You'll find His way almost always different than what you thought the solution had to be.

When you ask for help, and then later realize: "Wow! My situation has been dealt with—*that was perfect*"—but not in the way you'd ever have thought possible, remember to thank God for it. So many times, He has come in to solve my issues—and in ways I could never have imagined! I've said, and continue to say so often: "*How that turned out was perfect!*" Yes, "*perfect*"—that's God's signature—and it's also a milestone to tell you that you're on the right path, and drawing closer to Him. So push forward then, with more perseverance then ever; you have His attention.

"With all your heart, say your own 'little backyard prayer.'"

Everyone will have a different starting point, and different reasons to start their pursuit—a situation in your life that will hopefully have you decide to become a "God chaser." All too often, I believe, it's tragedies and untold hardship that eventually causes a person to cry out to God. I hope my story will save you from waiting until a day when tragedy strikes, and you have nowhere else to turn. When you decide to pursue Him, I'm convinced that you'll experience unfathomable rewards. Nevertheless, if you do decide to wait until that day when you're sick and tired of being sick and tired, overwhelmed with grief, remember what you have read in this book; and with all your heart, say your own *"little backyard prayer."*

God is very approachable. Be real. Be humble and compassionate, be relentless; and ensure that your heart is honestly in pursuit of God. Seek Him, not the rewards; they'll come automatically if He is the object of your desire. But He will not be used as a device to get you the rewards! Additionally, be bold and be yourself. Then, armed with those tools, your probe into the mysteries of God, the supernatural and the reason for your life will soon have your own spell-binding and amazing story unfolding.

You should know that my most powerful encounters with God happened during the time I was *not* attending any sort of church. Nor was I of any particular denominational belief at the time. My understanding of the Christian faith was, at the time, an actual mix-and-match of many church teachings. Some churches can be a major discouragement on your journey, which was certainly the case for me. Looking back however, they each in turn taught me some valuable things I needed to know; so today, even though most had disappointed me at the time, I now have instead an appreciation for every one of them. Yes, I understand now how God used every one of those churches and persons to play an important role in my development and journey. Your journey is not about them; it's about you.

> *"My most powerful encounters with God happened during the time I was not attending any sort of church."*

It's important to know that our personal encounter and subsequent relationship with our Father in heaven is not the church's responsibility. Rather, that responsibility rests with each one of us individually. Because your parents may not have taught you this, is no excuse. The Bible reminds us that *"The heavens declare the glory of God; the skies proclaim the work of his hands"* (Psalm 19:1). It's therefore my own sole responsibility to pursue God, not that of my parents and not that of Christians or churches. God made things obvious enough that anyone with a little common sense can realize and see the *intelligent design* involved in creating the universe, as well as the intricacies of the world we live in.

We were created with enough intelligence to know that we are not here because some so-called "singularity," created from nothing, exploded and then became a rock that eventually evolved into a monkey that happens to be your ancient relative. That man has come to believe and teach that absurdity, indoctrinating our children with nonsense, is certainly evidence of what the Bible warns us about in Revelation 12:9, *"The devil...the one deceiving the whole world."* My point, again, is this; I alone am responsible for my fate, in the same manner that you were made smart enough to be responsible for yours. I'll use a blacksmith's (my second Dad's) expression to say, "Don't believe that evolutionary hogwash." Andy

> *"I have honestly testified and shown you that a relationship with God is an actual one-on-one relationship with God, and nothing less."*

One final point on this matter: the closest relationship one can have with God is not through any church, nor any act, work, tradition, or sacrament. Those can all be very important things; but I have honestly testified and shown you that a relationship with God is an actual one-on-one relationship with God, and nothing less. In the Bible it is written: *"Draw near to God, and he will draw near to you"* (James 4:8). Additionally, the more sincere and persistent your pursuit, the further you'll be able into enter His inner sanctuary, as I was. And you must know that I'm still pursuing Him, to go deeper.

> *"Demonic powers of deception are exceedingly more than I could ever have imagined."*

I'm obligated to reiterate what my life journey helped me discover about the demonic forces we are dealing with on a day-to-day basis. Demonic powers of deception are exceedingly more than I could ever have imagined. It was only because I lived through thirty years of torment and thousands of deceptions that I finally understood the power of the enemy to the level that I do. I cannot imagine that any person on earth has the capacity to defeat such a powerful and deceptive force. Most have no idea that they are even under its influence!

As I had mentioned, the Bible warns us in Revelation 12:9 that *"The devil, or Satan, the one deceiving the whole world—was thrown to earth with all his angels"*; and I, for one, can bear witness, after them attacking me for so many years, that the statement is true to its core. Therefore, it's important for you to realize that a passionate pursuit of God is going to involve unwanted company. The devil in no way wants to see you get engaged in that activity.

Also know today that God will provide protection; but expect the fiery arrows to come, because they will. He promises in 1 Corinthians 10:13 *"He will not allow you to be tempted more than you can take. But when you are tempted, He will make a way for you to keep from falling."* So keep your eyes and mind open for the escape that you will always be offered.

Because my eyes have been opened to the extent they have, and my spirit has experienced first-hand both the demonic and the angelic supernatural, I have a profound realization of how deceived and off-track mankind is. I easily recognize the fact that it's absolute foolishness for anyone to think that there's any wisdom aside from what God gives us. Unfortunately, what mankind does with that wisdom is most often questionable; and yes, for their own ungodly purposes. For mankind, the ultimate "shock and awe" will come when this all-powerful God reveals Himself to this world; every knee will not only bow, they will humble themselves and melt in worship. That's guaranteed!

"What you cannot see is not only more real; without a doubt it created what we do see."

One other thing that all this has unmistakably shown me, and that I hope you have come to realize, is that outside my body (and yours) is another dimension, much more real and much more alive than the one in which we currently exist. Our brain allows our spirit to control our bodily functions, nothing else; and once we depart from our body, our mind (our person) has no more purpose for our brain. That's a given; I've been there hundreds of times. What you cannot see is not only more real; without a doubt it created what we do see, which is only temporary.

In conclusion, we humans have a problem in humbling ourselves enough to ask for help; and it was only the continual torments that eventually beat me into submission, and had me finally become humble enough to ask for help. James 4:6-7 says, *"God opposes the proud, but gives grace to the humble." Submit yourselves therefore to God. Resist the devil, and he will flee from you."*

Me sharing in this book what I found out about the enemy was reason enough for him to concentrate so much effort in trying to stop me.

> *"The devil will be relentless in his efforts to lead you to set other priorities in your life."*

Know this: the devil will be relentless in his efforts to lead you to set other priorities in your life, or to suggest that none of this is relevant; so you have to be equally relentless, and persist in asking God (the Holy Spirit) for help. And He will faithfully come alongside to assist you. Just as red-hot steel is hammered and shaped to become an instrument in the hands of the black- smith, so are we shaped by our pursuit to come alongside a most holy and powerful God, so that He can use us to be His instruments. Yes, He will use what is imperfect; but He will see to it that we are hammered and shaped and made fit enough to come alongside Him. The Bible says that we'll go through trials in our pursuit; but it also says that we'll be provided a peace through it all. Only God has the capacity to defeat Satan; so without His help, believe you me, you'll be on a dead-end road—and I say that with certainty.

> *"The most amazing discovery I've made is that we can **all** have a one-to-one relationship with our powerful and almighty Creator."*

The power and magnificence of God is awe-inspiring, breathtakingly beautiful and indescribable; that's my privilege to share, only because of my passionate and persistent pursuit to stand alongside Him. My hope is that you have come to understand that the most amazing and rewarding discovery I've made is that we can *all* have a one-to-one relationship with our powerful and almighty Creator. What He's done for me, He will do for you—and more.

Does God want to be personally involved in everyone's life? Absolutely! That was His intention to begin with; and anyone who actively becomes a God-chaser will experience God in such wonderful ways! Acts 10:34 says, *"I now realize how true it is that God does not show favoritism."* Which means that what He has done for me, He will do for you. He doesn't have favourites.

> *"So the bottom line is: God didn't create a fool; that's a personal choice."*

I had often said, *"Well if God exists, then why do these terrible things happen?"* Back then, I had all kinds of excuses to not pursue God, and that was just one of them. However, after experiencing God as I have, I fully realize that, yes, He has given us intelligence, but absolutely nothing in comparison to His. He created the universe you can now look at. For us to try to understand everything about God is complete foolishness on our part; we haven't been given that kind of mental capacity, nor do I believe for a second that we need it. He has, however, given us enough smarts to realize that He does, in fact, exist; and because of that, the Bible states in Psalm 14:1 *"The fool says in his heart, 'there is no God.'"* So the bottom line is: God didn't create a fool; that's a personal choice.

If, at this point, you still have some doubts about all this, that's not a surprise; but let the truth of this scripture raise a red flag for you: 2 Corinthians 4:4 says, "*Satan, who is the god of this world, has blinded the minds of those who don't believe. They are unable to see the glorious light of the Good News. They don't understand this message about the glory of Christ, who is the exact likeness of God.*" The good news I'm sharing with you is this: you can have those blinders removed and be given new sight in the same manner that I was. That process and experience was absolutely amazing and truly the ultimate miracle! Who would ever of thought such a transition of the mind could be possible?

> "*The moment you transition to the other side you most certainly will believe what I've written in this book.*"

Pray that God opens the eyes of your heart, mind and soul; because one thing I know for certain: whether it be in this life or your next, the moment you transition to the other side you most certainly *will* believe what I've written in this book. Mark 8: 36 warns us; "*What good is it for someone to gain the whole world, yet forfeit their soul?*"

If hell is even remotely similar to what I had to endure periodically over thirty years, I couldn't imagine having to spend eternity under such torment; and Matthew 7:13 tells us that so many will choose just that: "*The way is broad that leads to destruction, and there are many who enter through it. For the gate is small and the way is narrow that leads to life, and there are few who find it.*" Are you going to bother yourself to be one of the few to find it? I can assure you of one other thing with certainty: when you find it, you will beyond a doubt know that you have found it, just as certain as you would be if you found a golden nugget.

"Finding it isn't difficult."   Finding it isn't difficult; a *simple back-yard prayer* will open that wonderful door (*the key*).

Even after having experienced what I have in my life, 1 Corinthians 2:9 promises that there is much more: *"No eye has seen, no ear has heard, and no mind has imagined what God has prepared for those who love him."* I've shared with you a glimpse of what has unfolded in my life; yet that scripture tells us that my mind still cannot imagine what is fully beyond those ancient doors. How amazing is that?

Let my last point be what *you'll find* written in Romans 12:2: *"Let God transform you into a new person by changing the way you think. Then you will learn to know God's will for you, which is good and pleasing and perfect."*

True to what is written, my *"little backyard prayer"* gave Him permission to *"change the way I was to think"* and thereby *"transform me into a new person,"* a wiser person and one who no longer experiences torments but instead wonderful miracles.

How amazing is that?

CPSIA information can be obtained
at www.ICGtesting.com
Printed in the USA
LVHW021606201020
669306LV00010B/1173